Cute and Fun
Kawaii Illustrations
Coloring Book

Corinne Larsen
Cover by Arjane Kinney

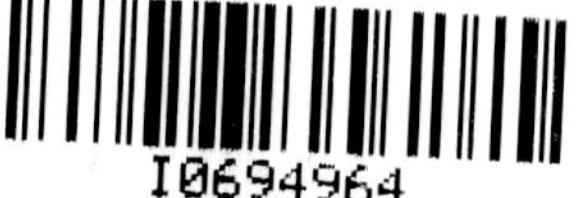

Cute and Fun
Kawaii Illustrations
Coloring Book

Larsen Falls Publishing

ISBN 9798864968383

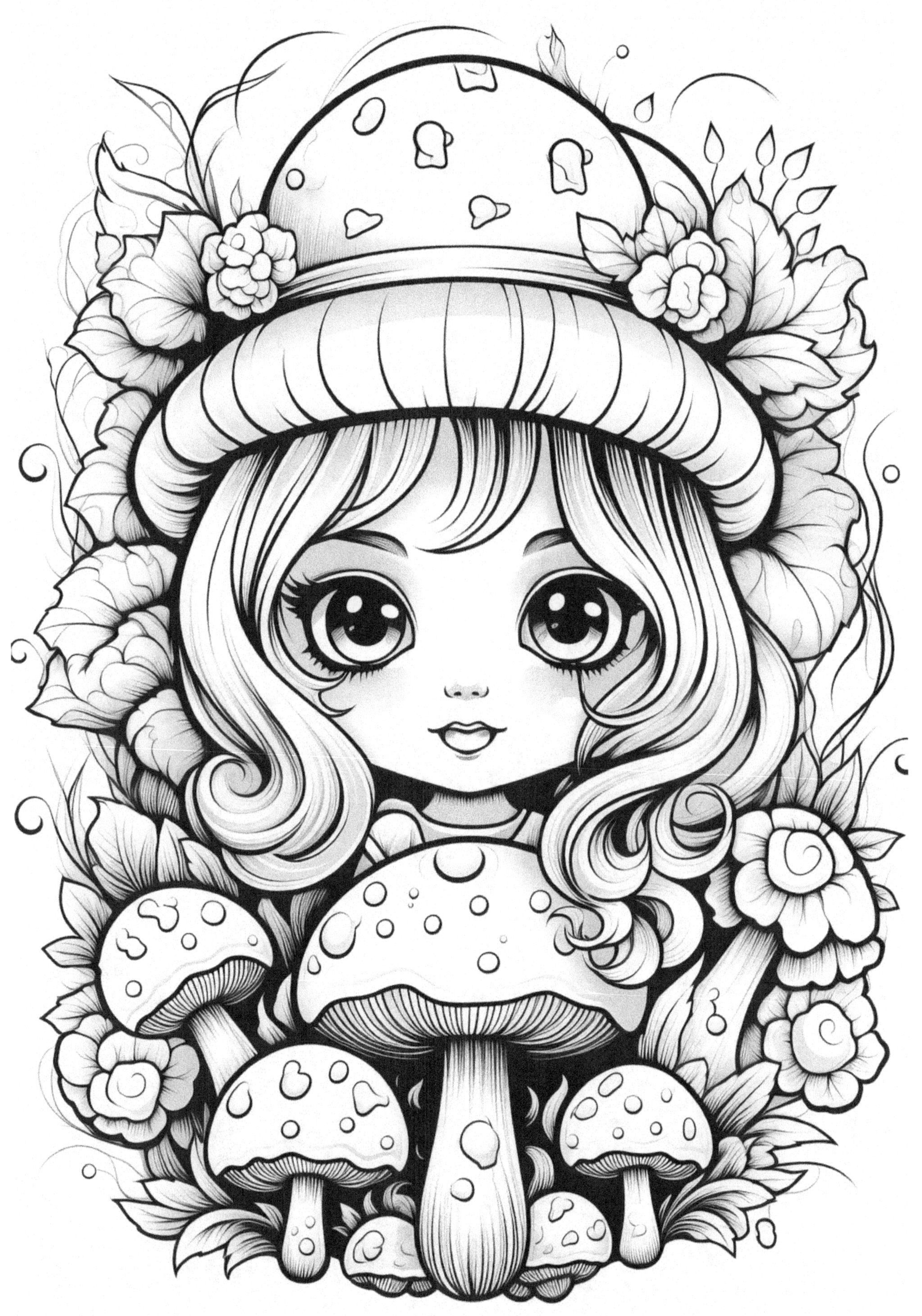

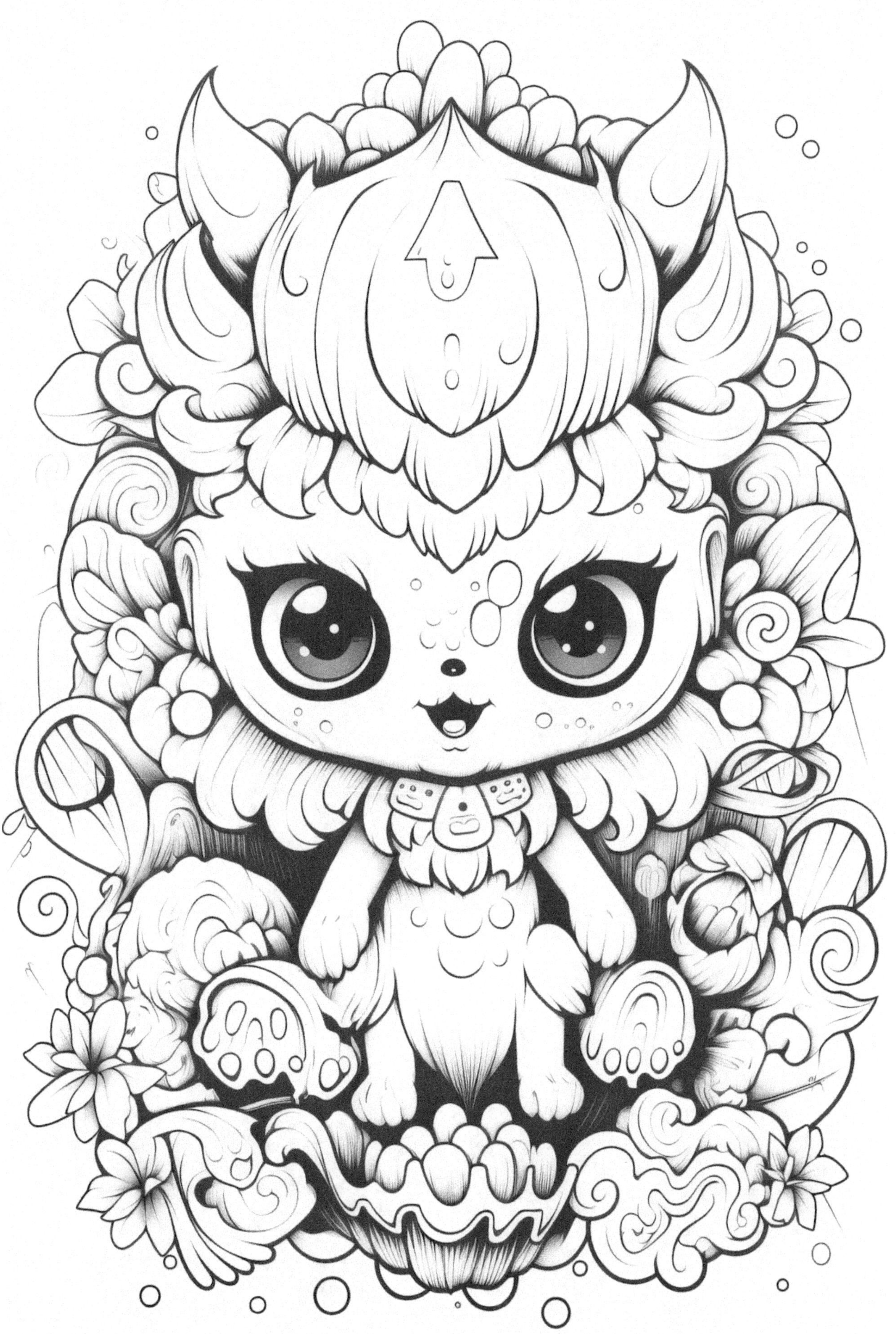

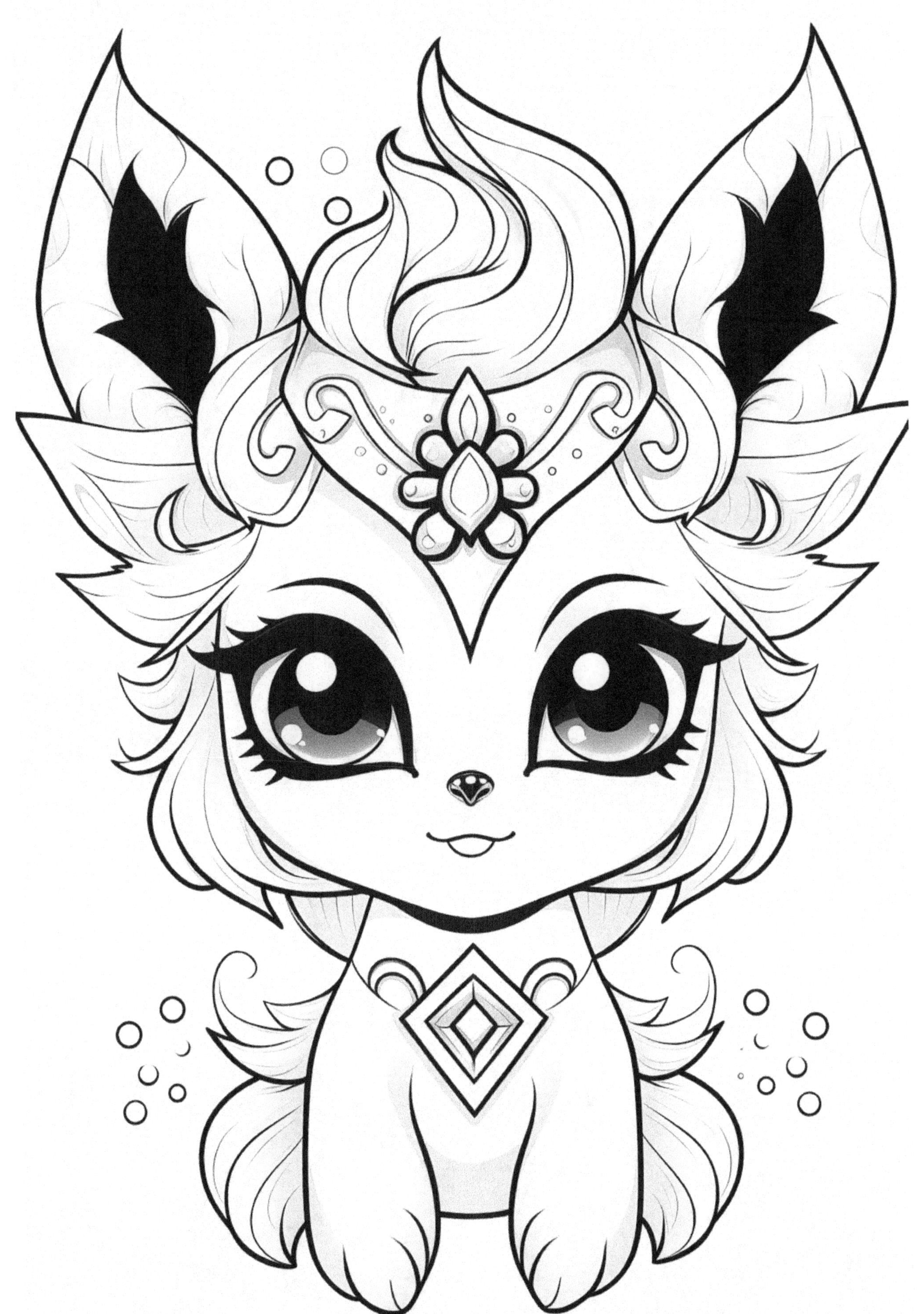

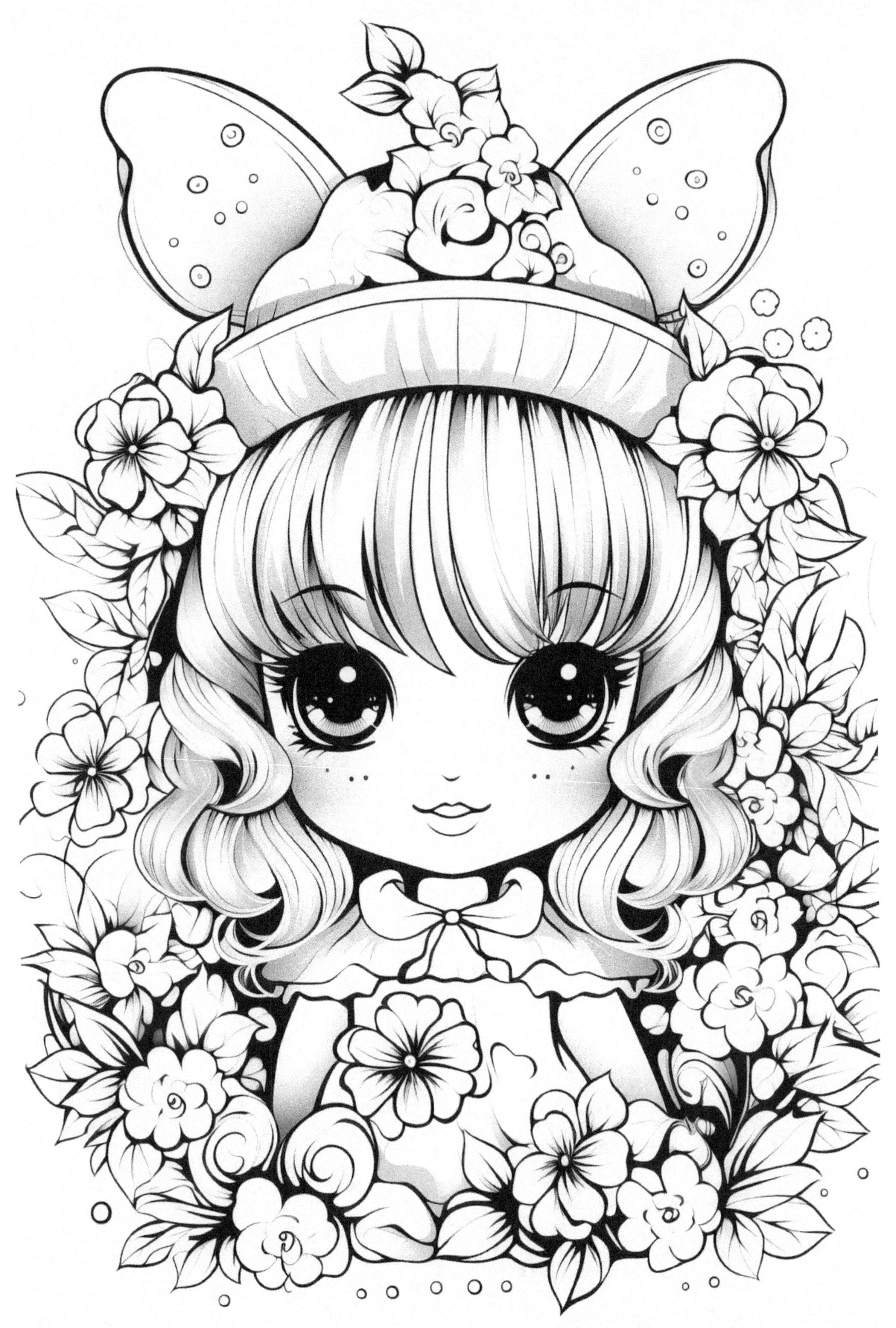

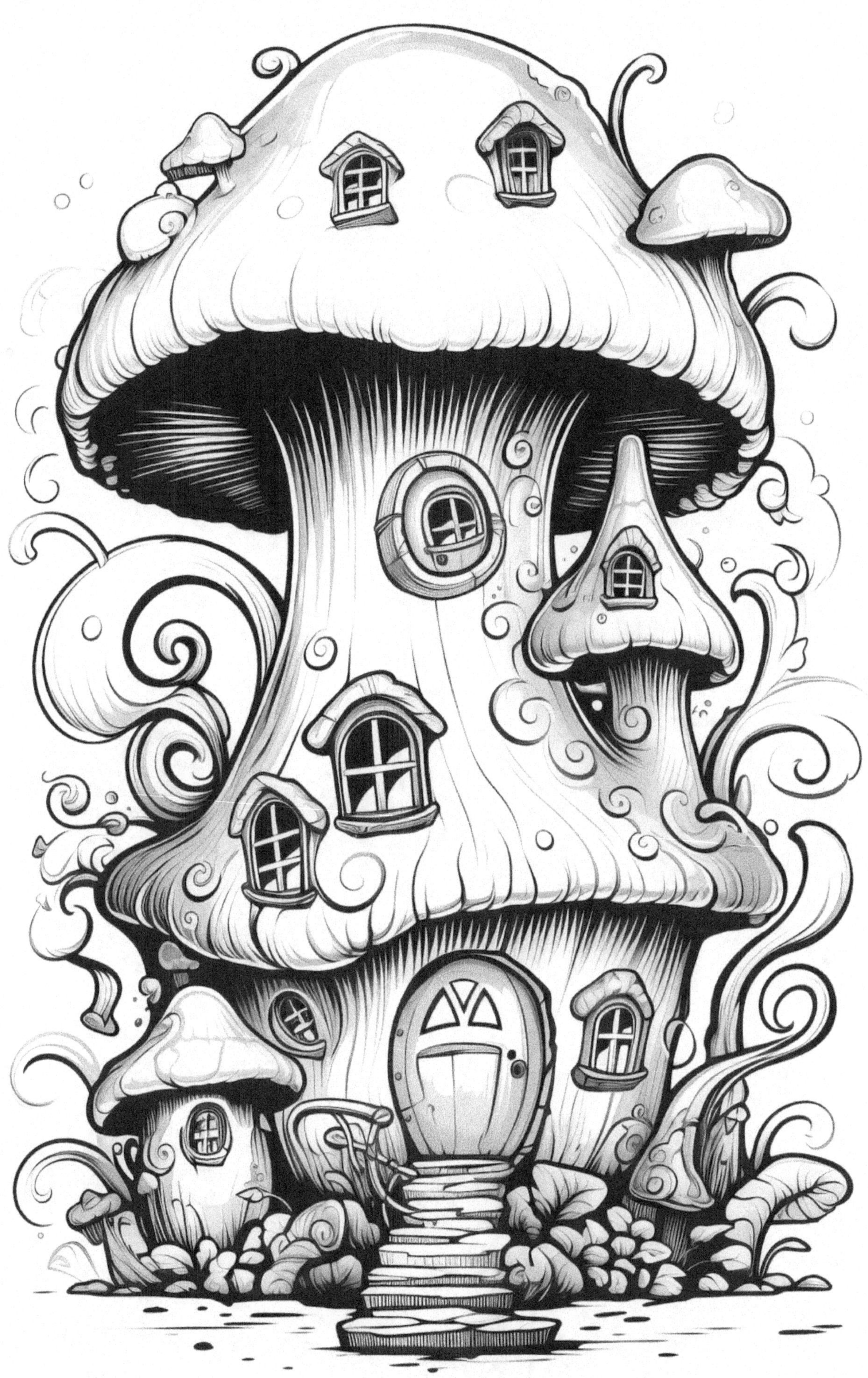

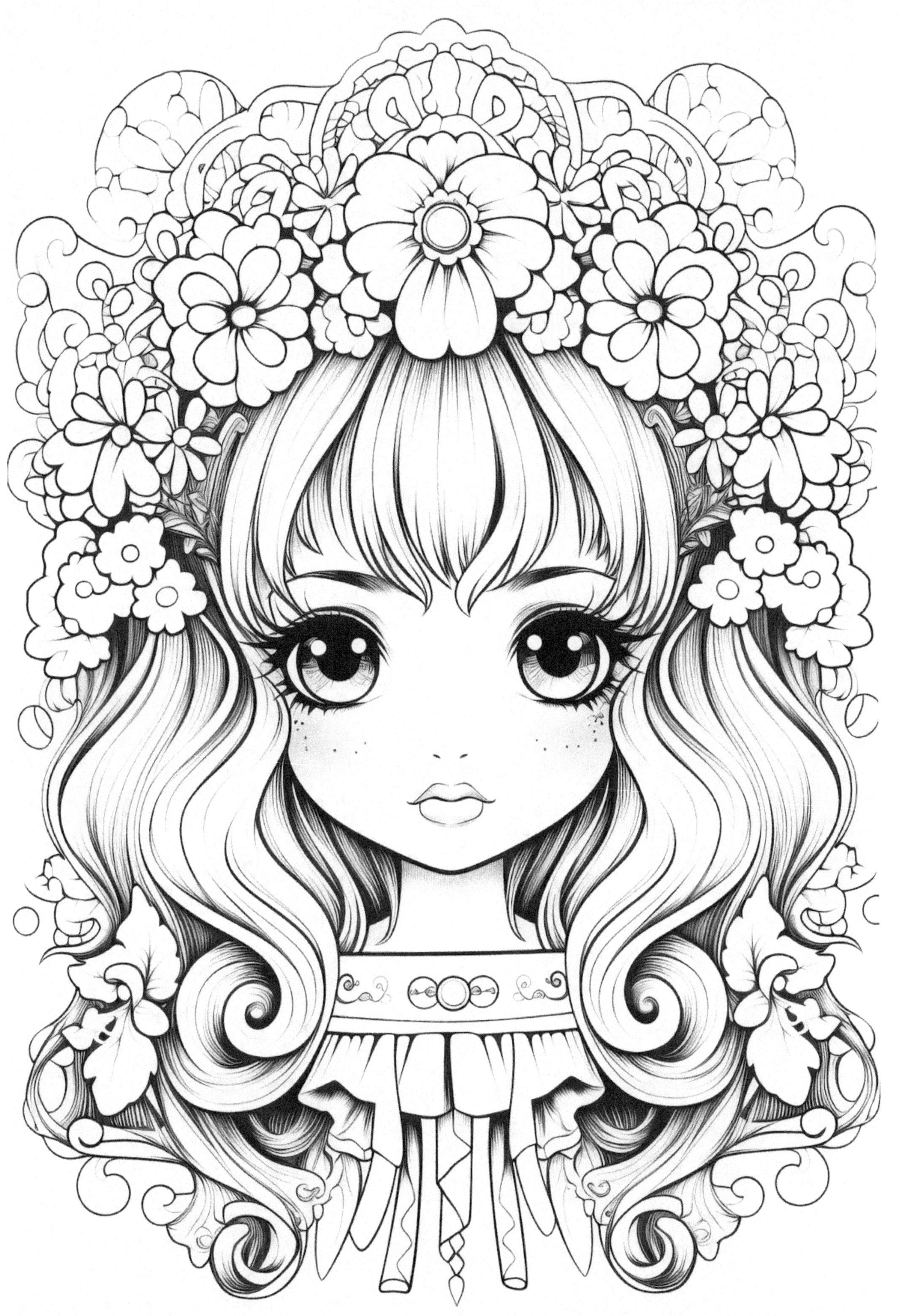

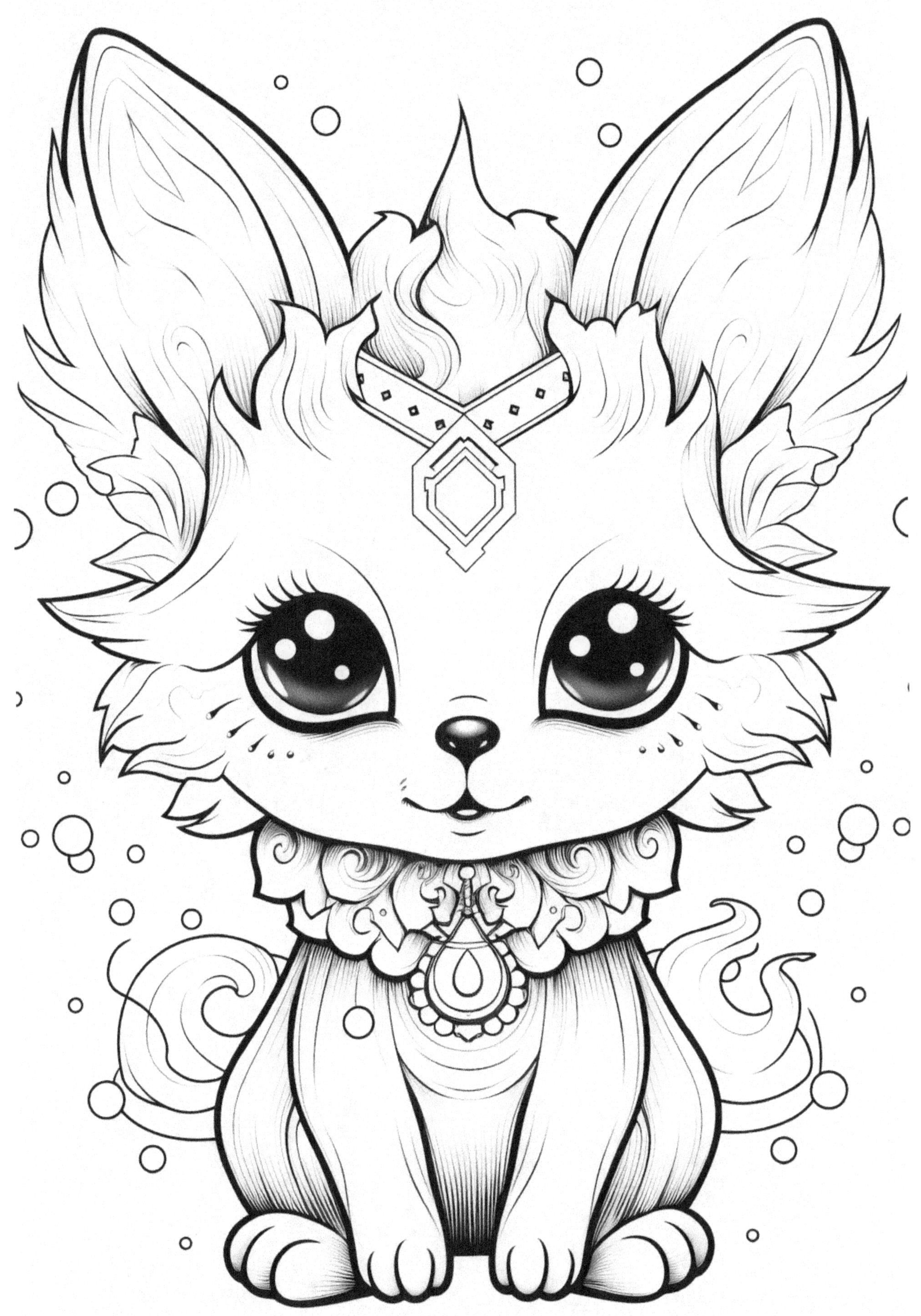

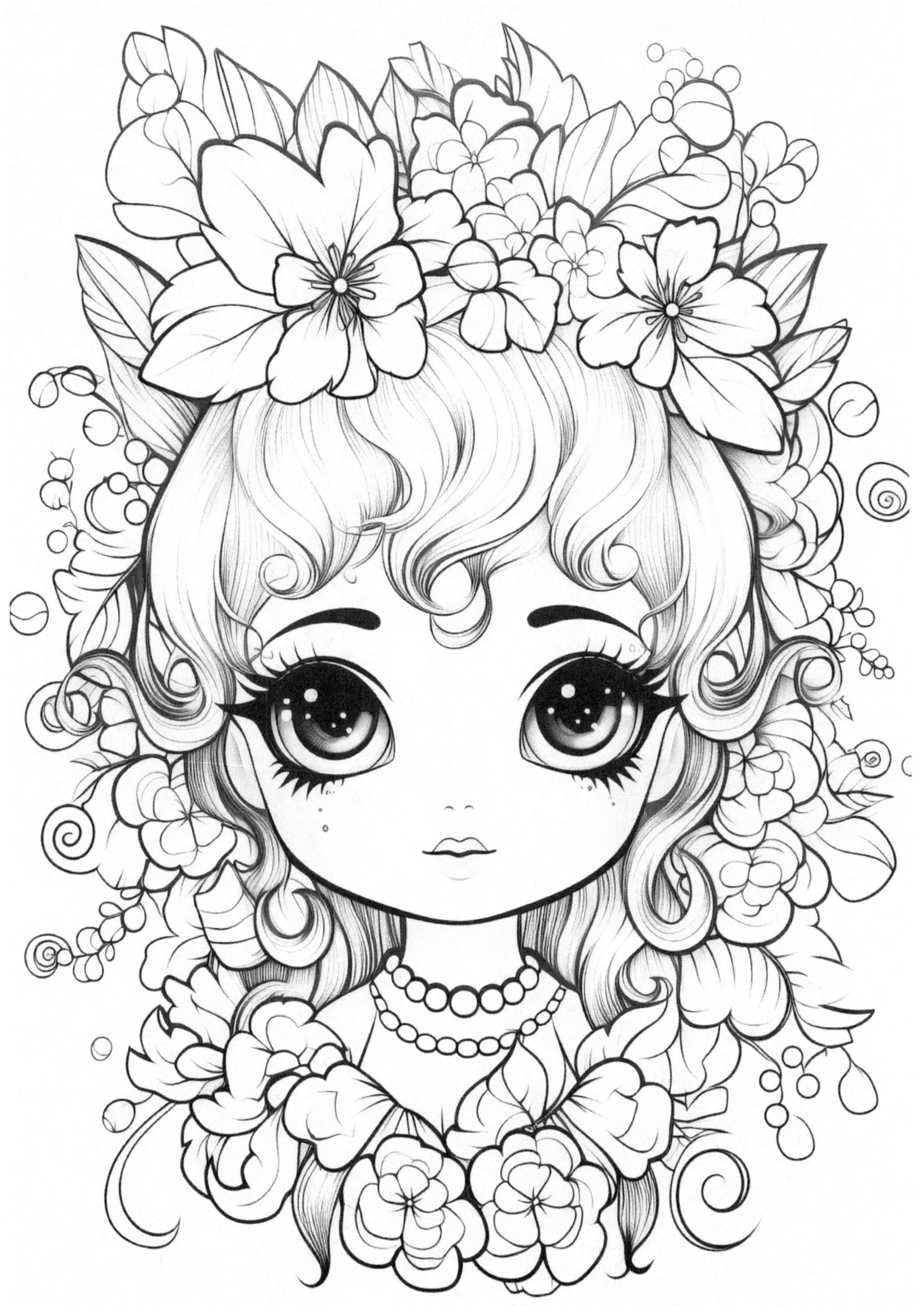

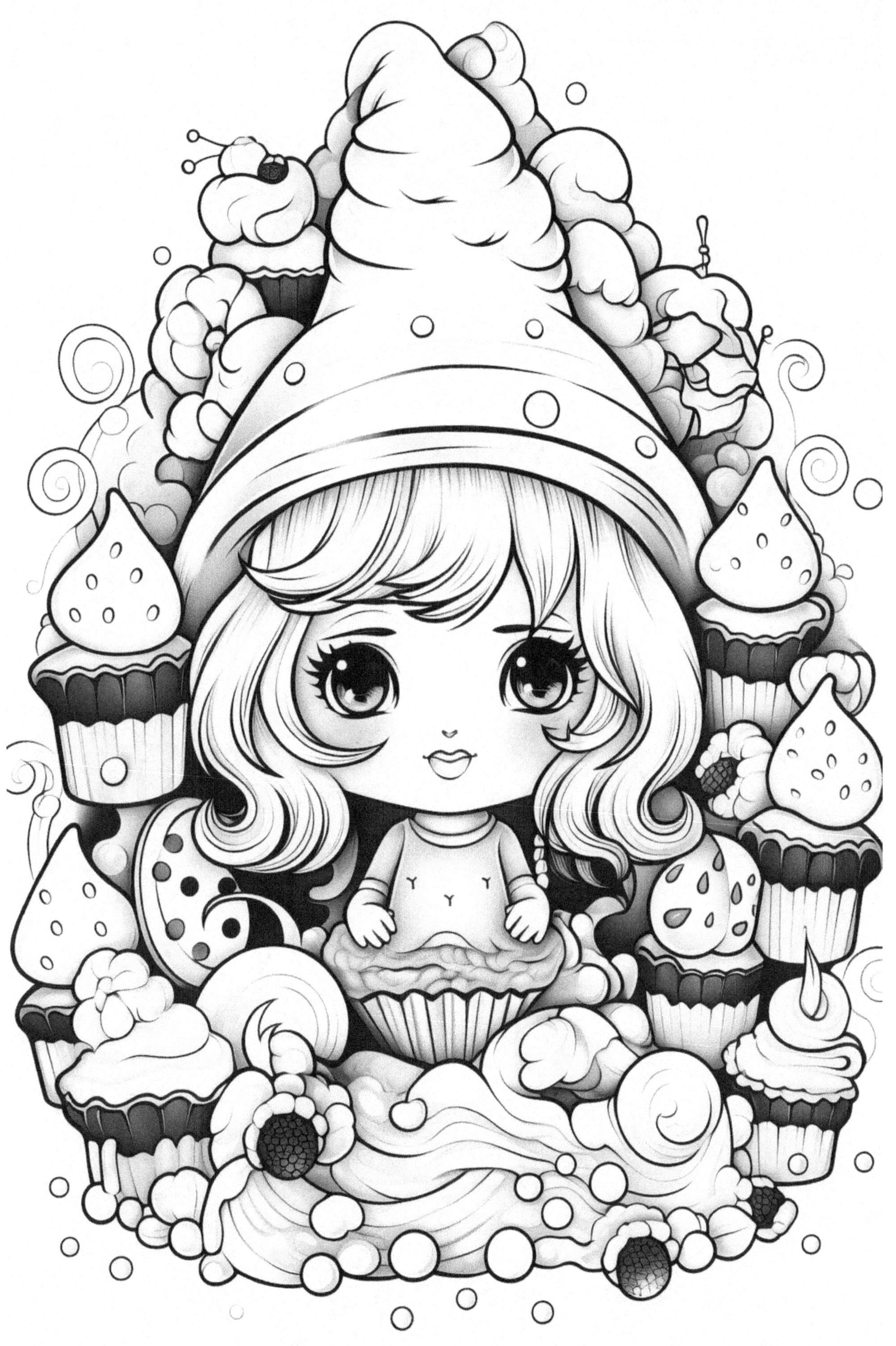

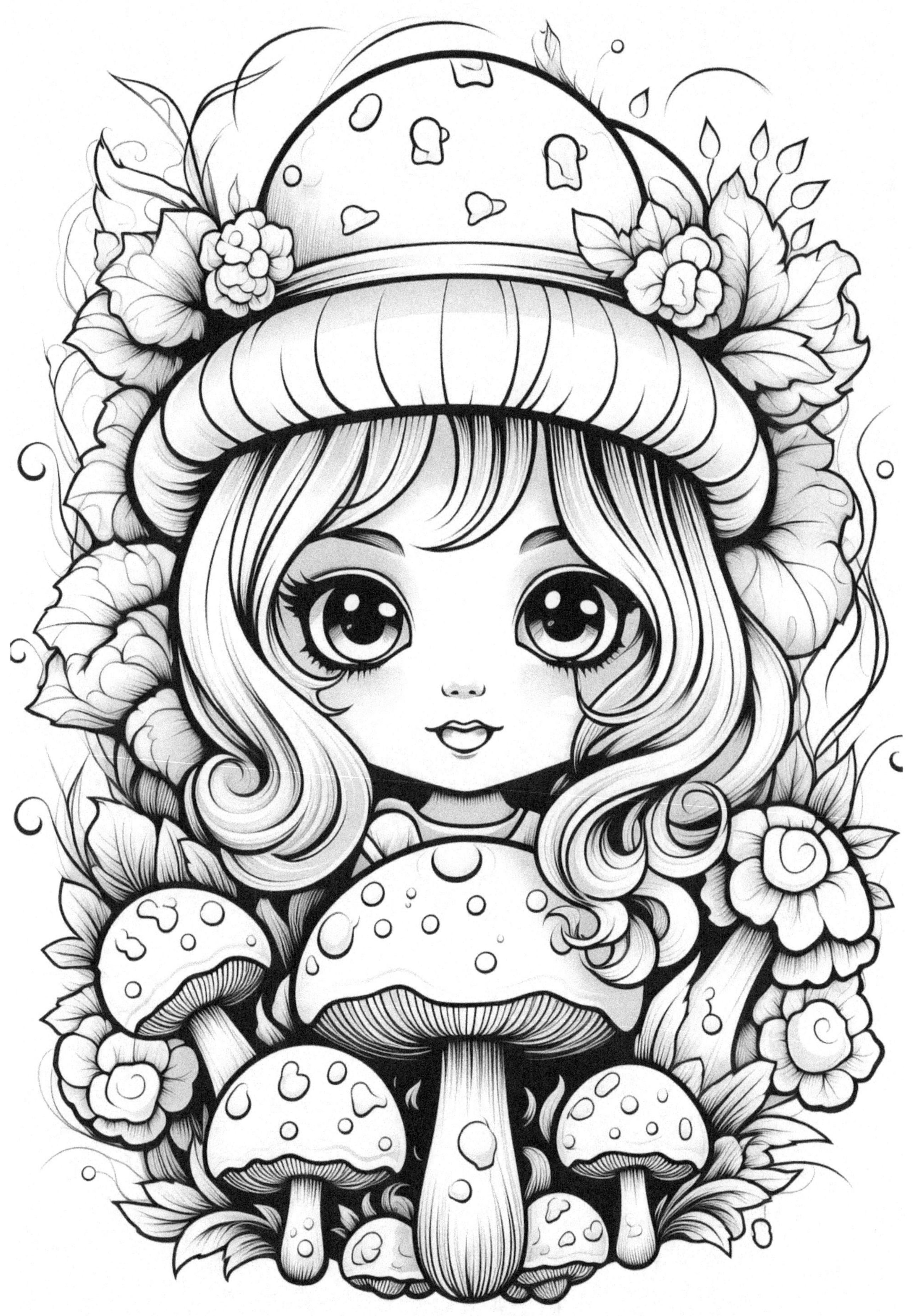

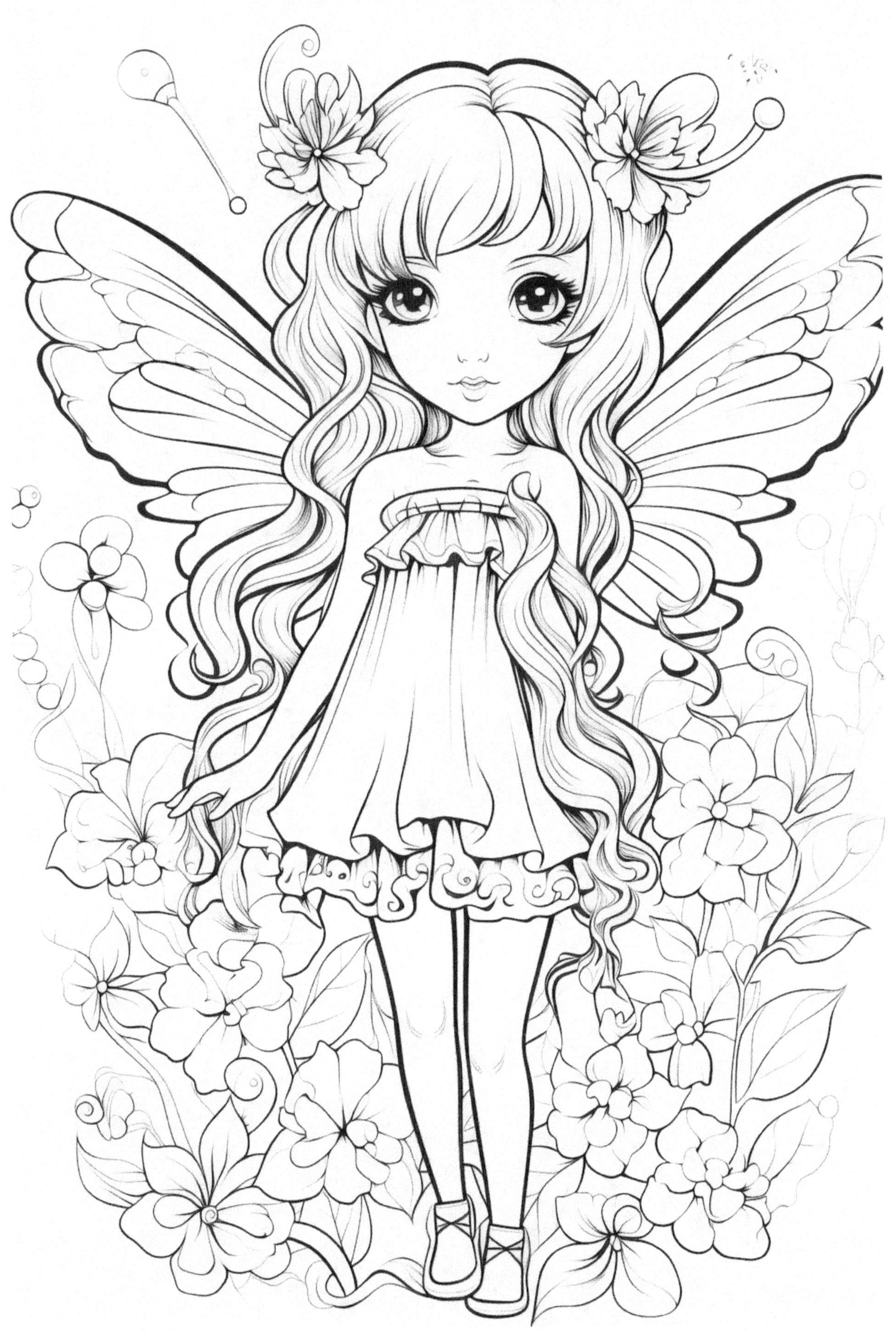

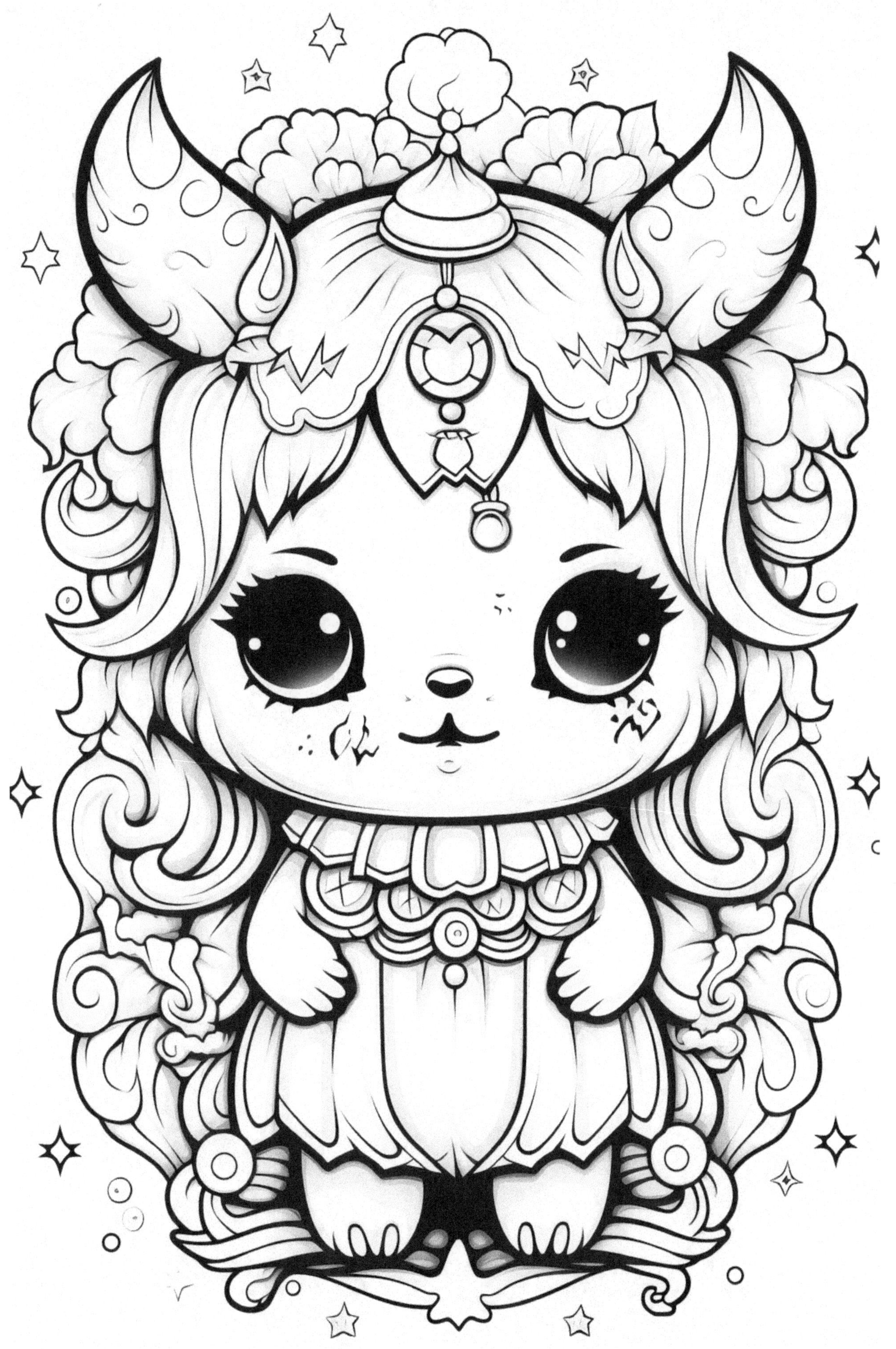

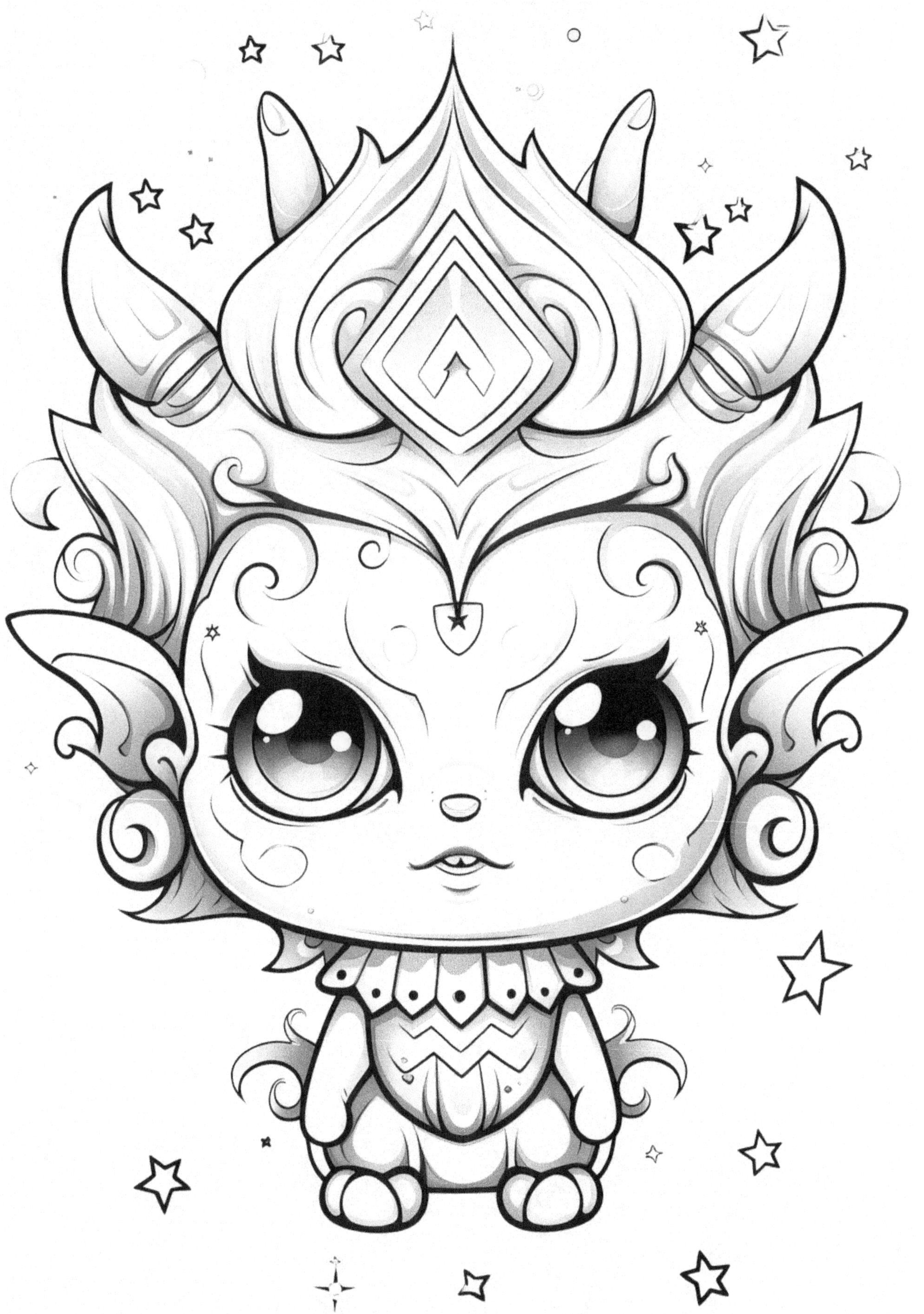

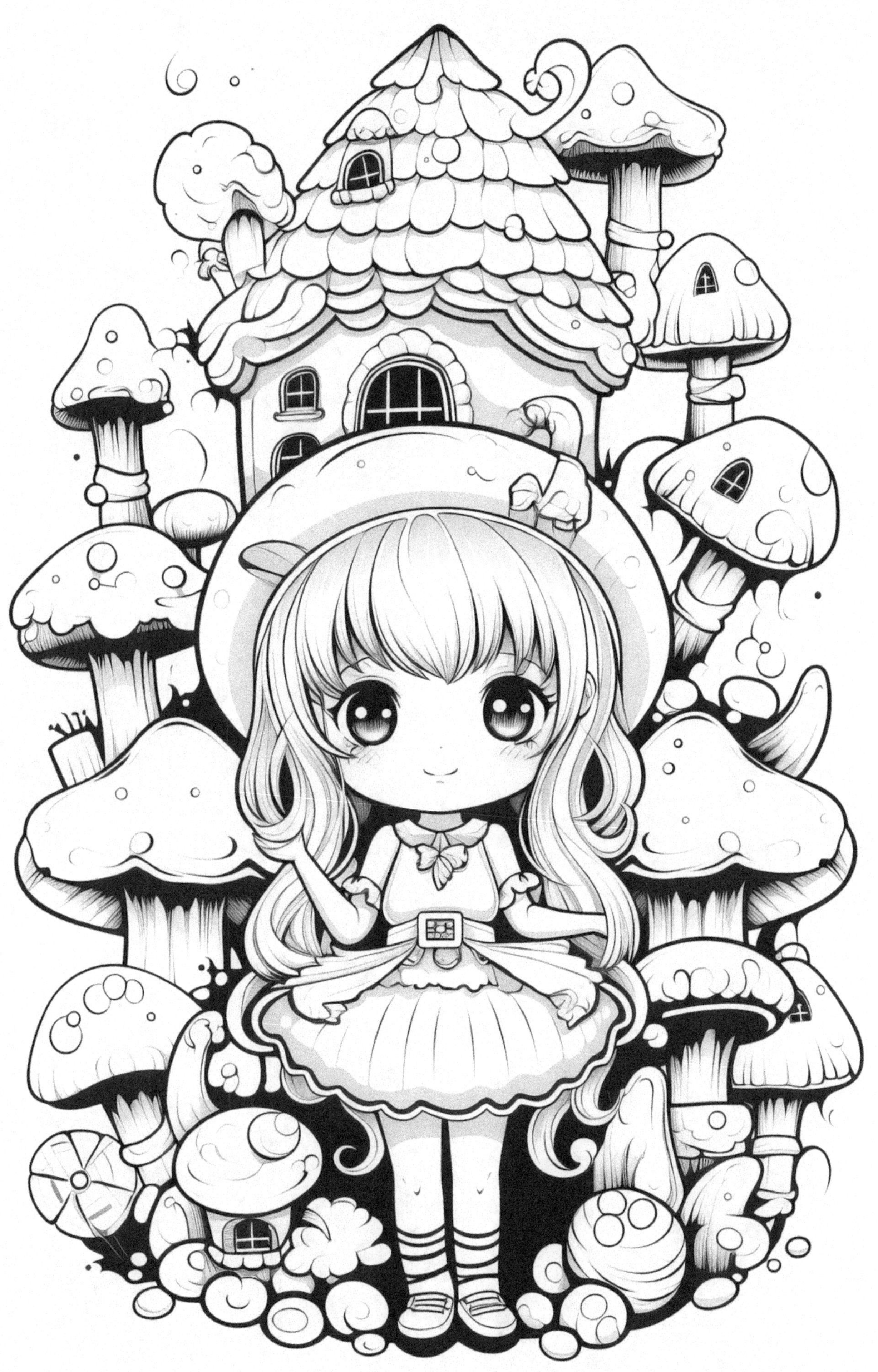

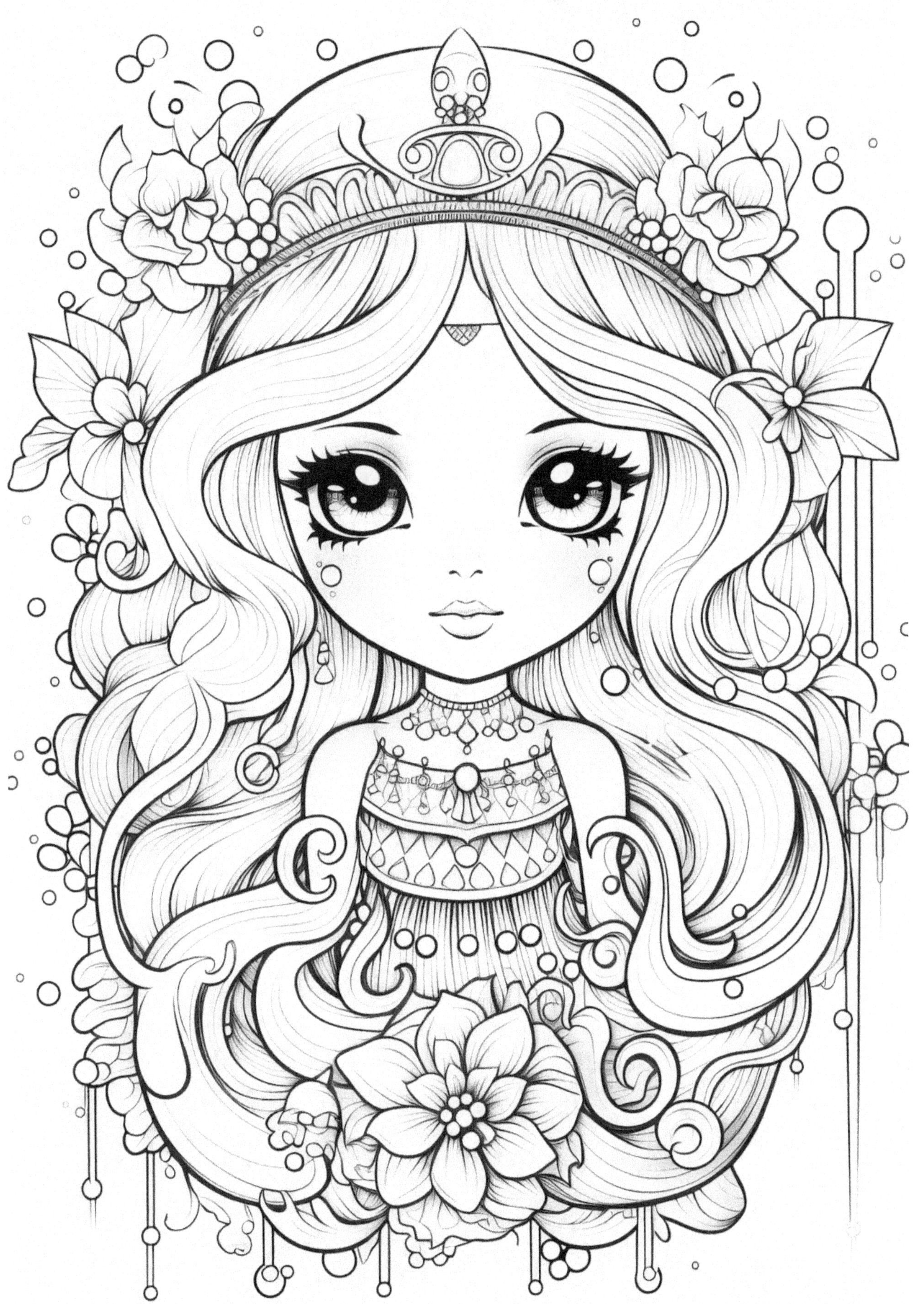

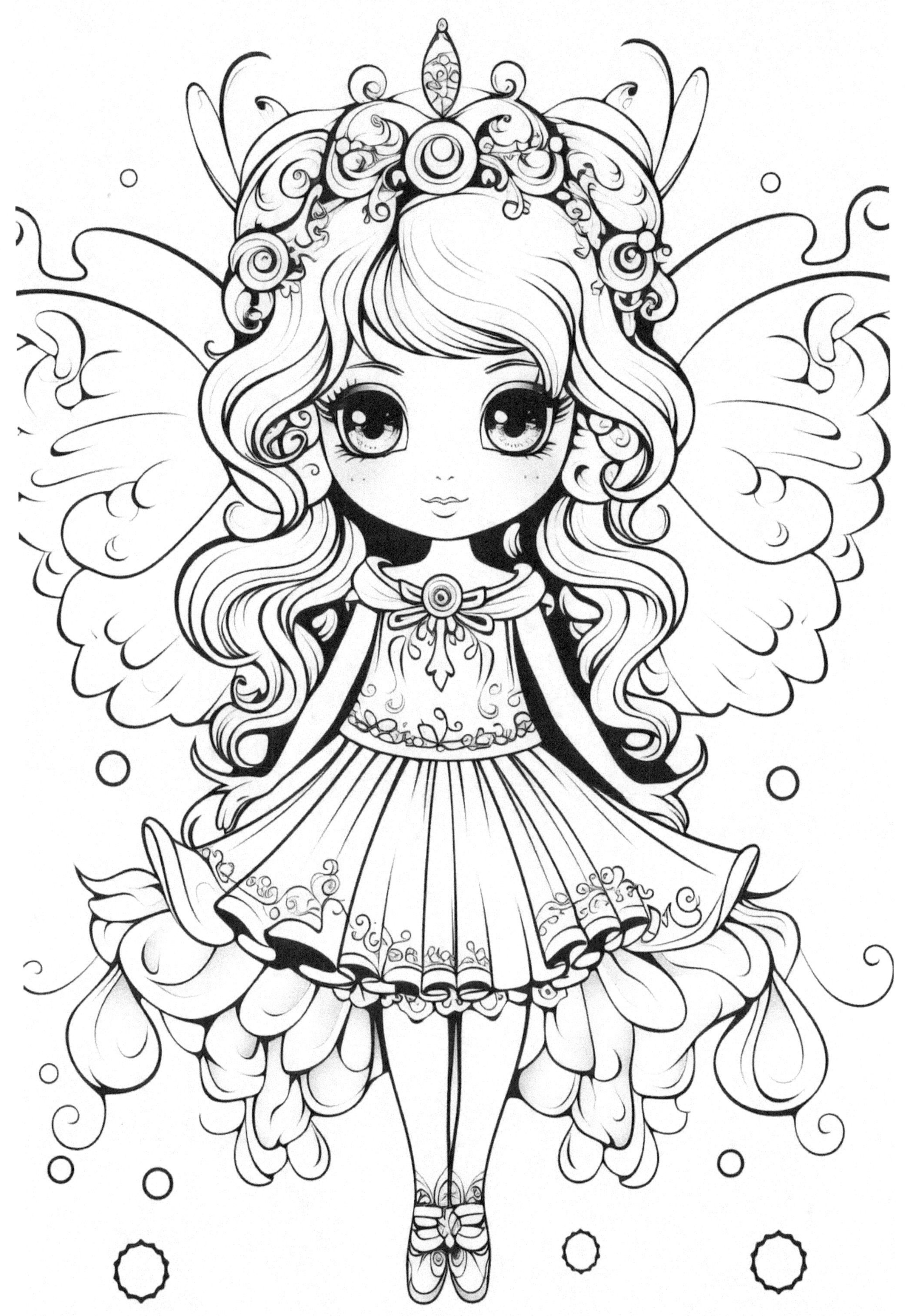

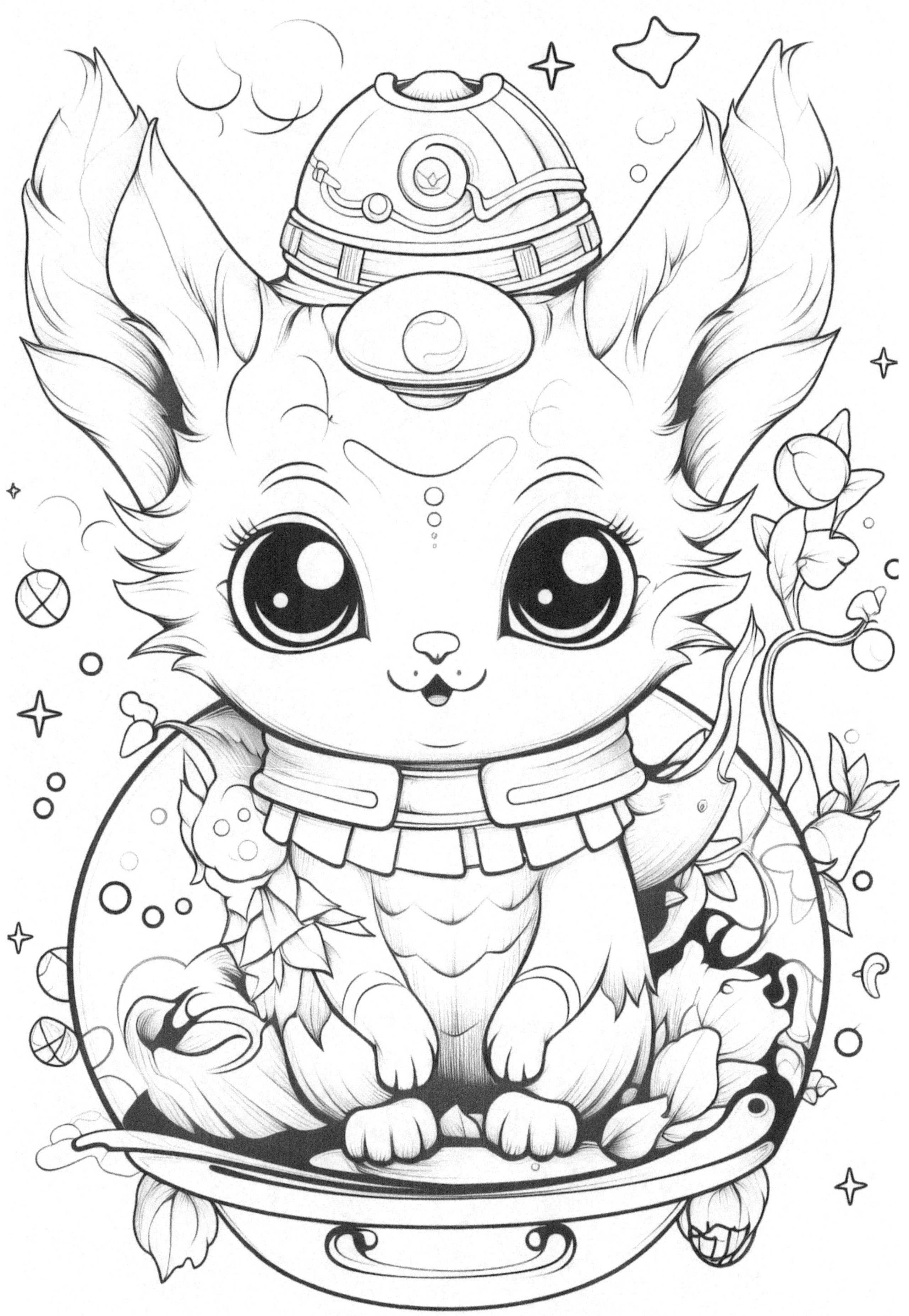

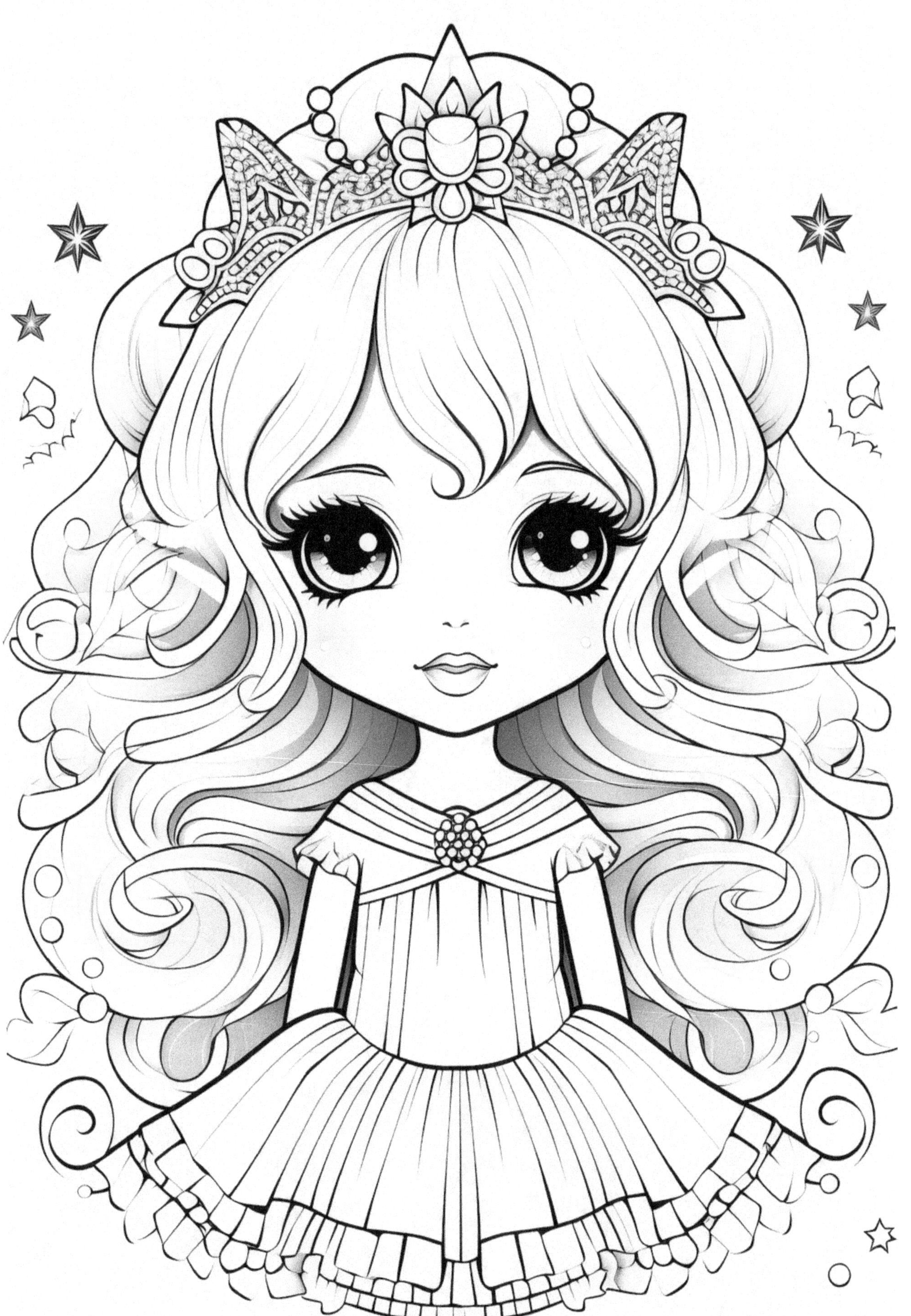

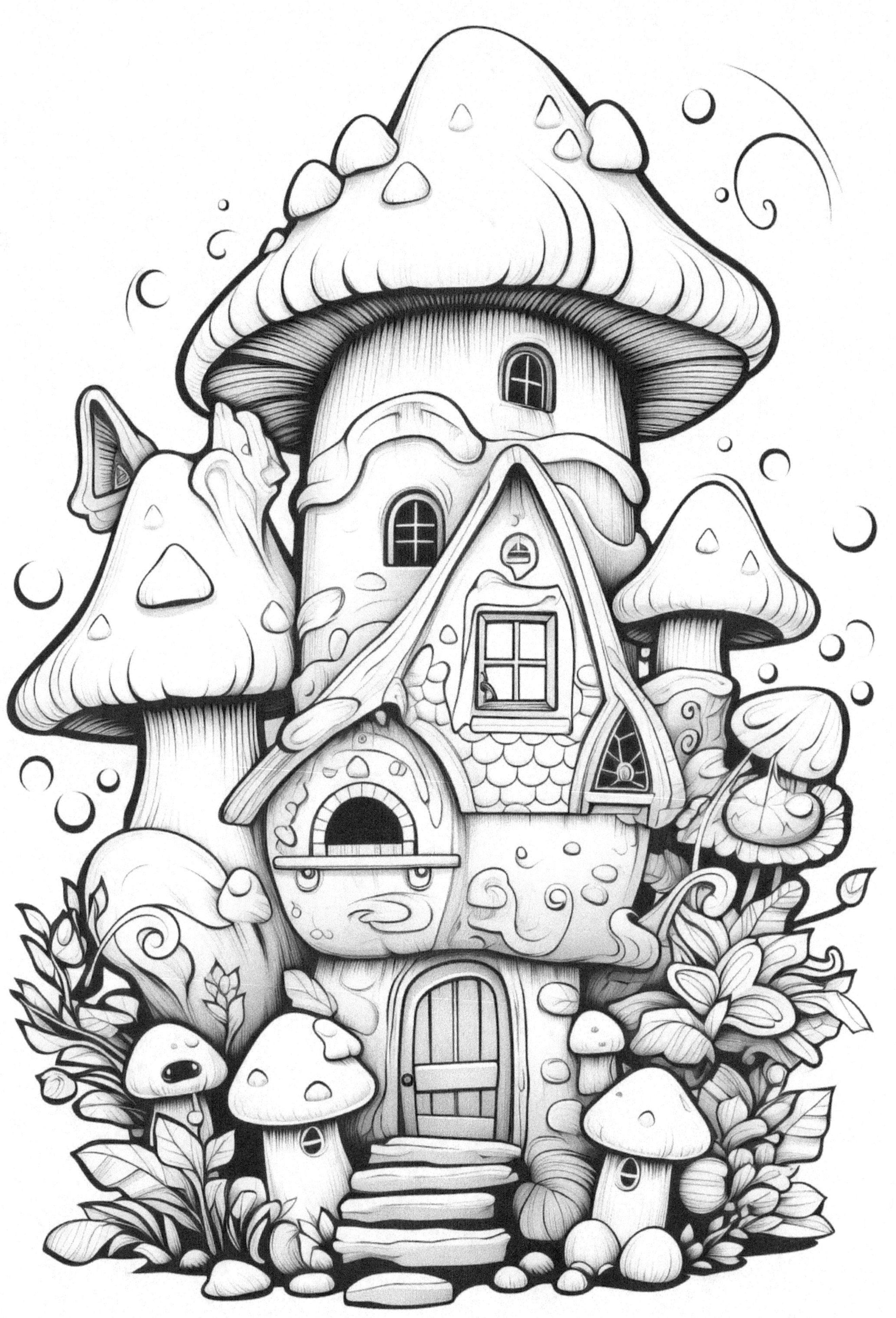

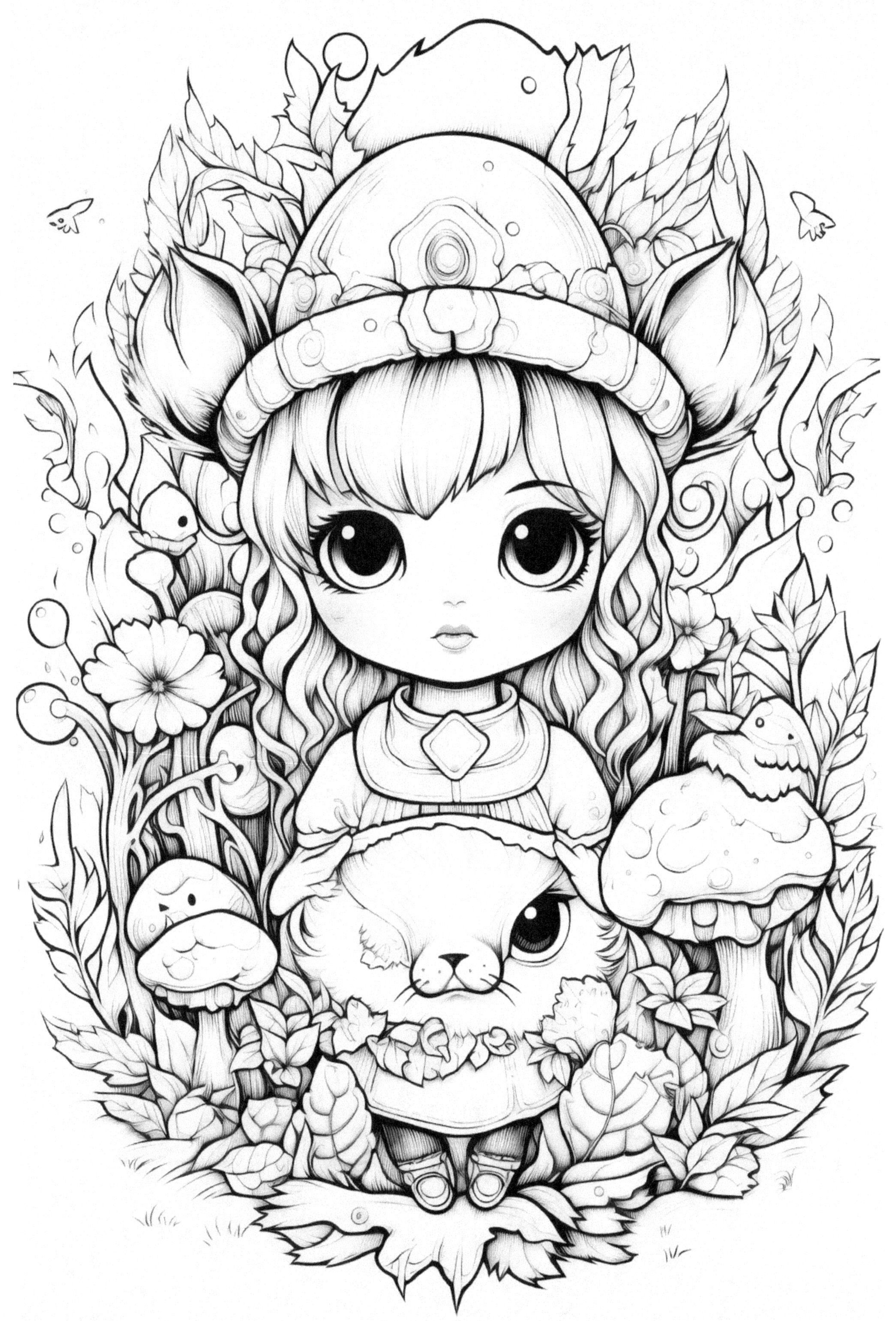

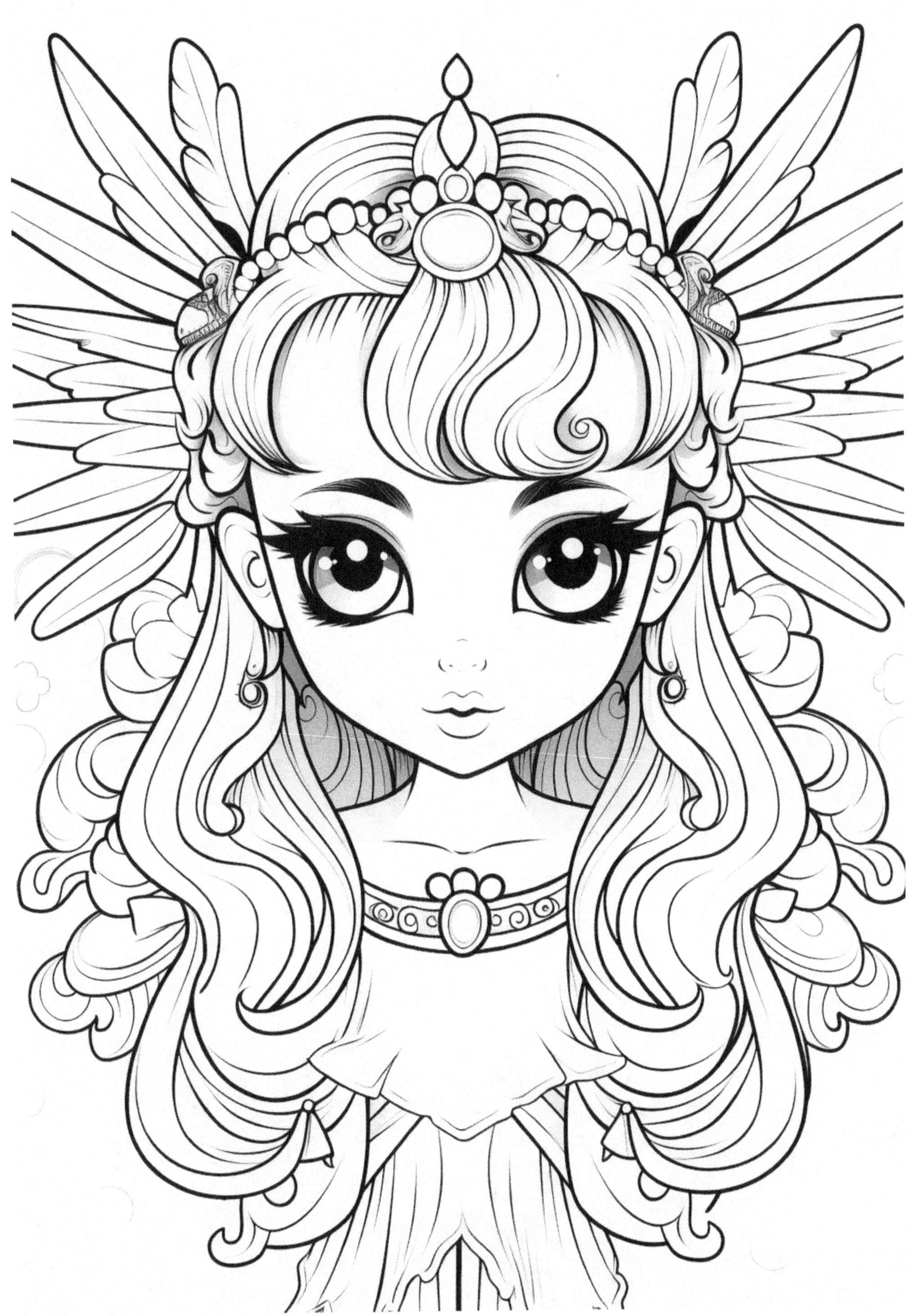

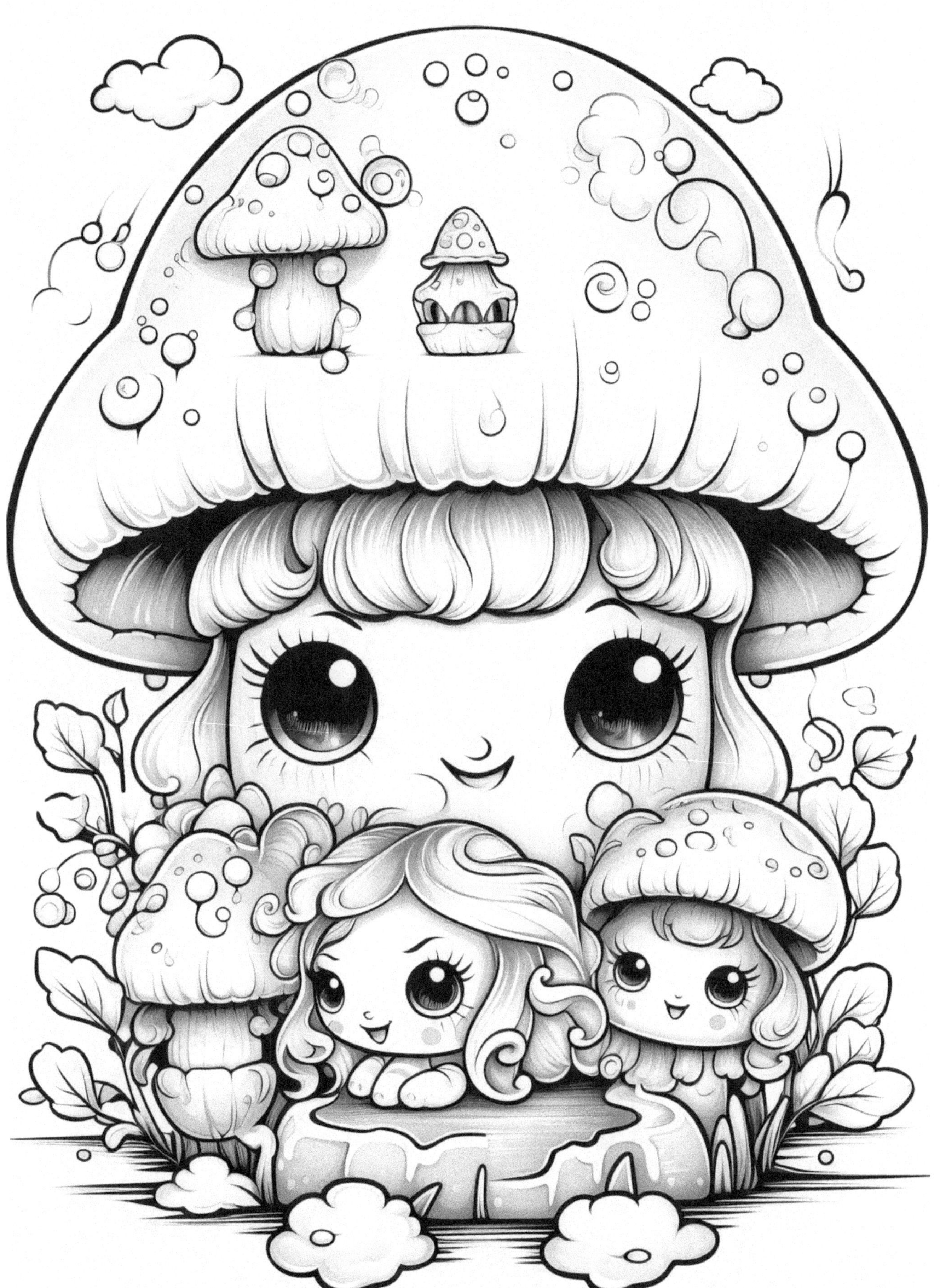

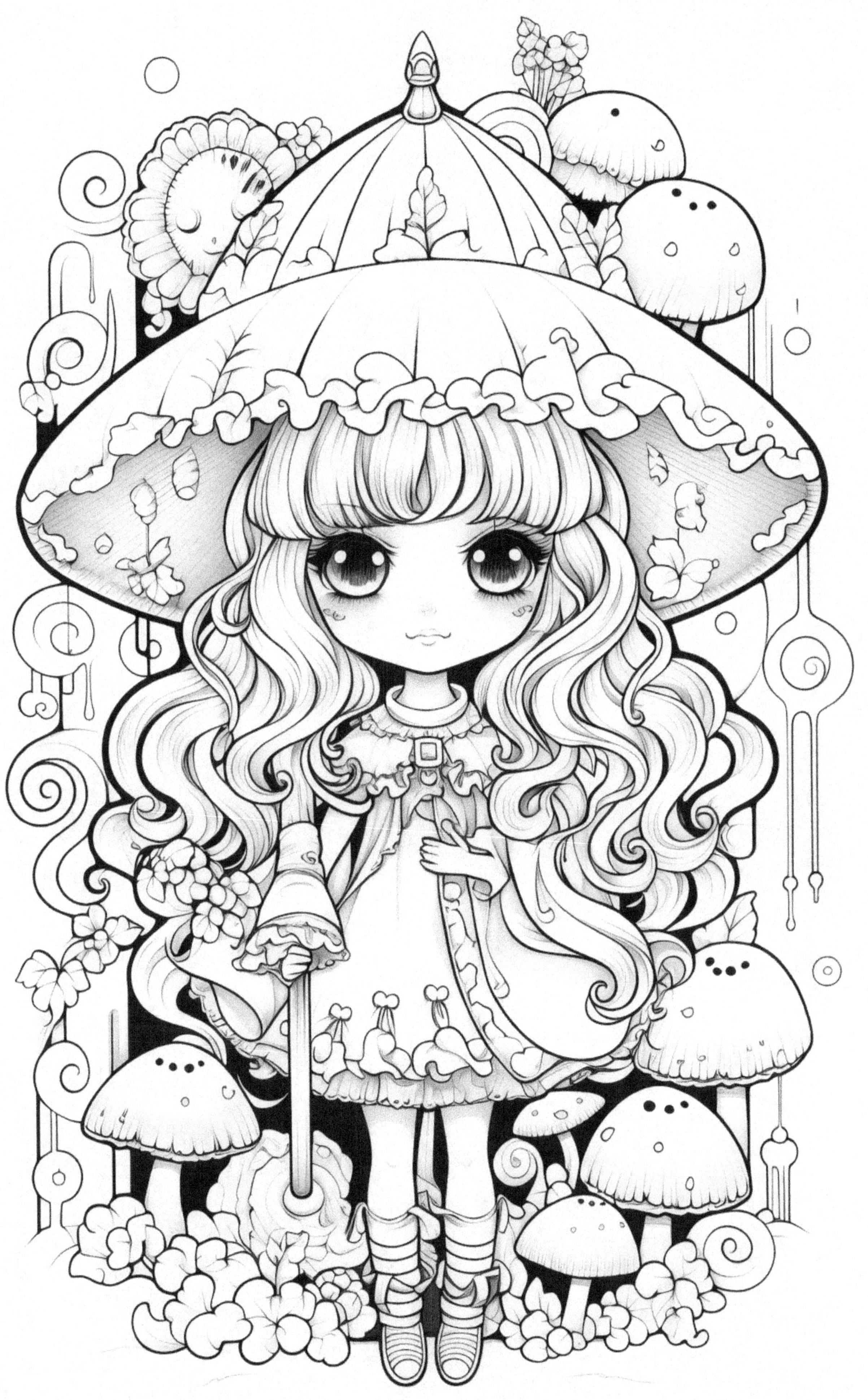

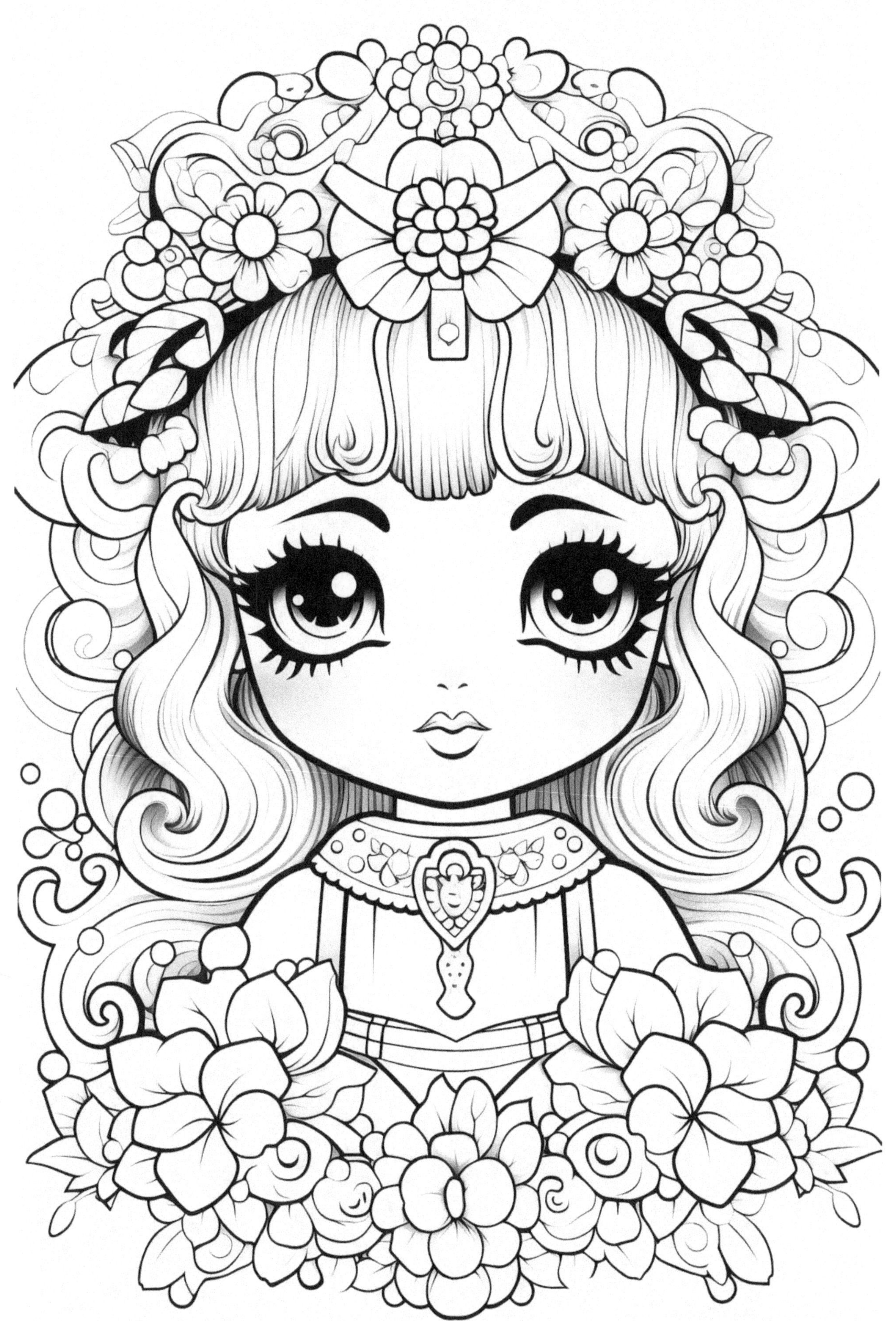

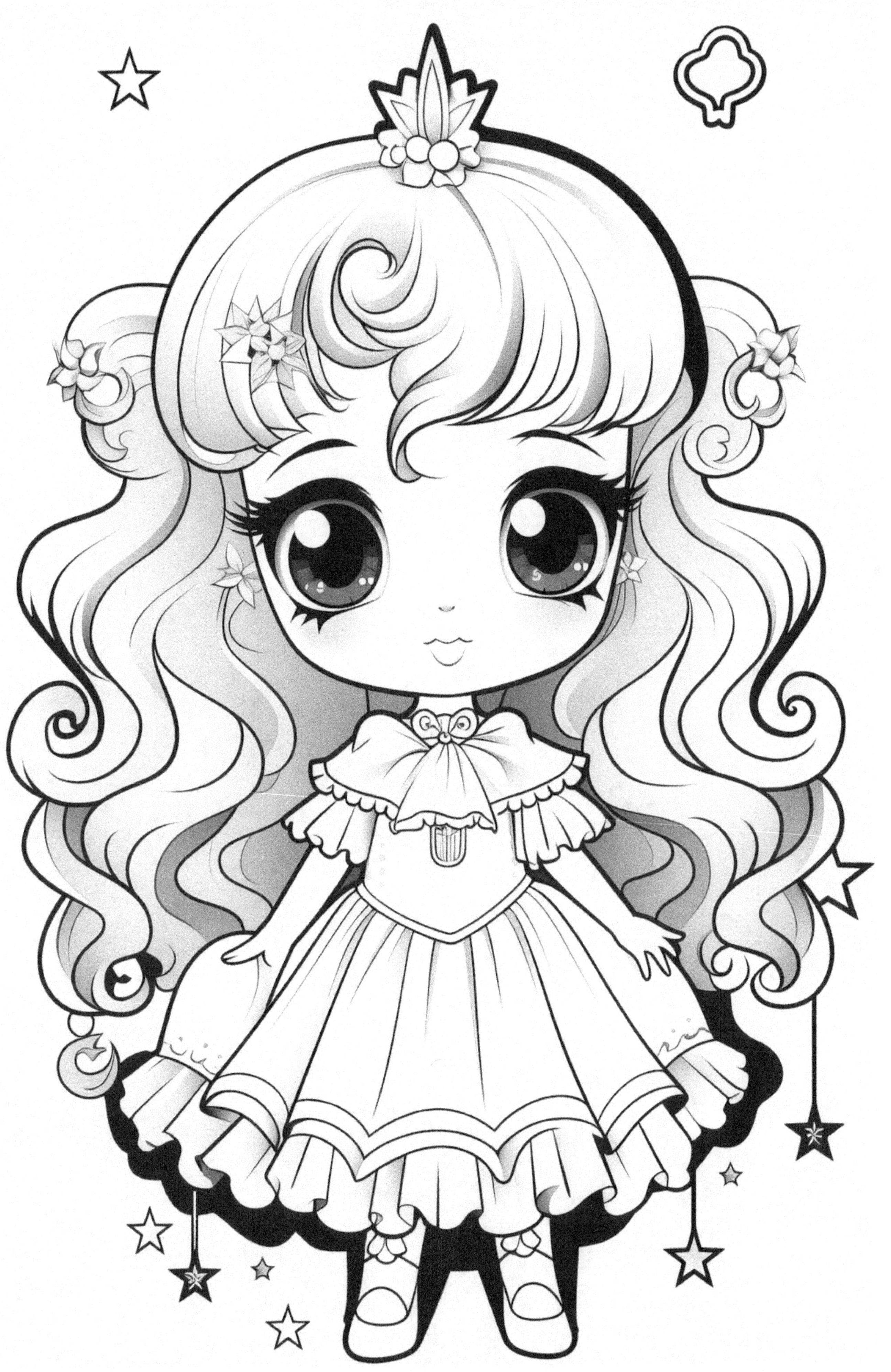

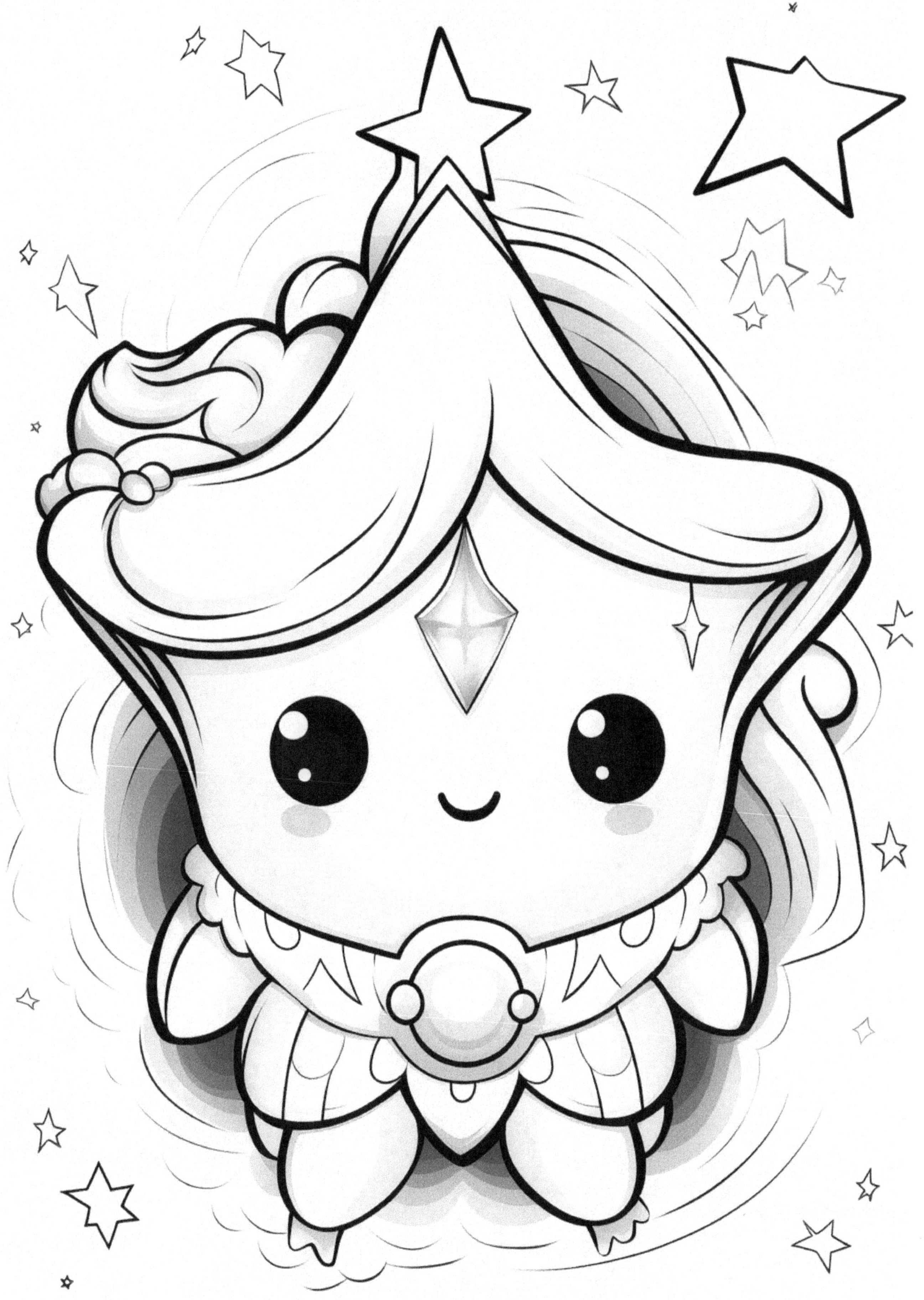

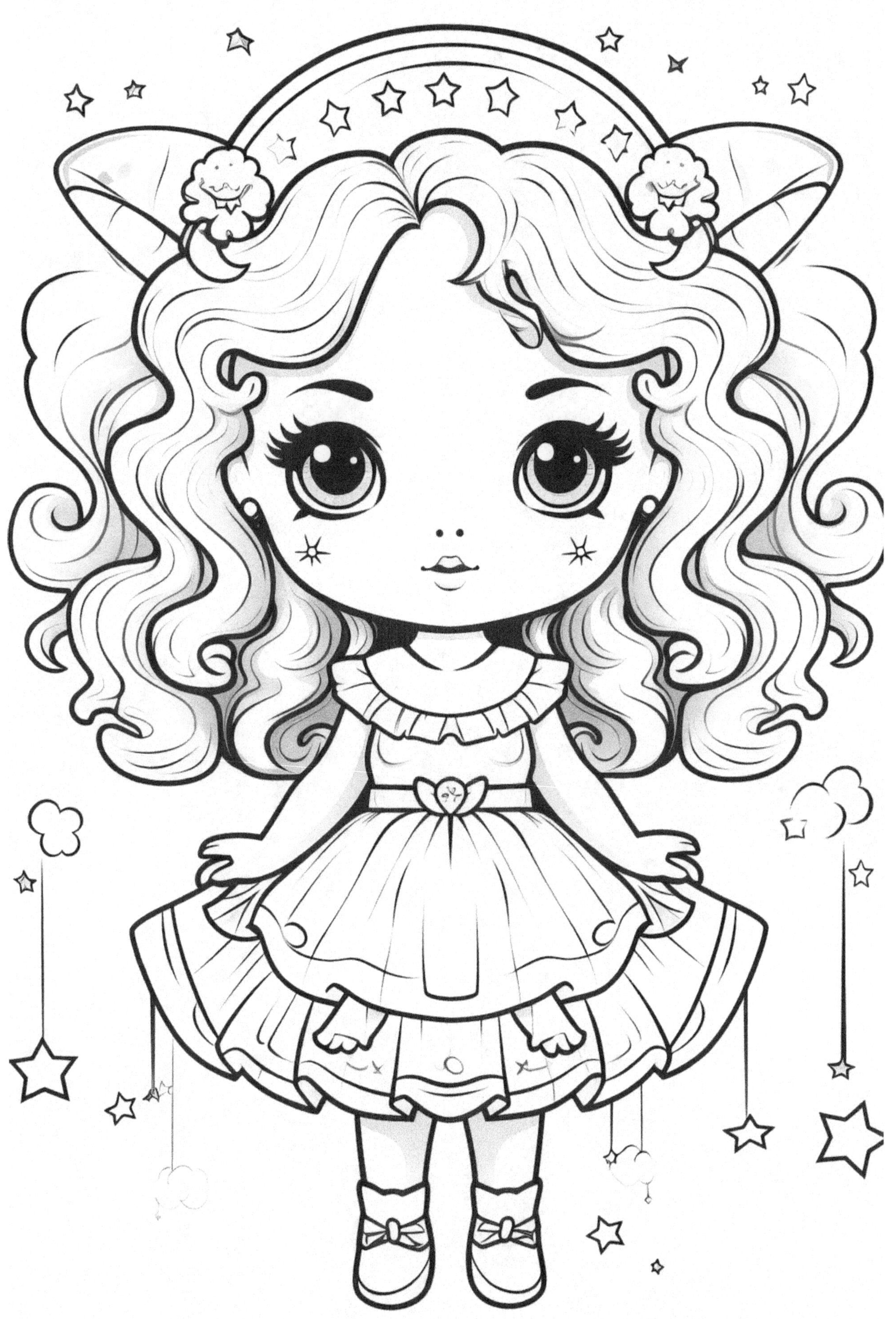

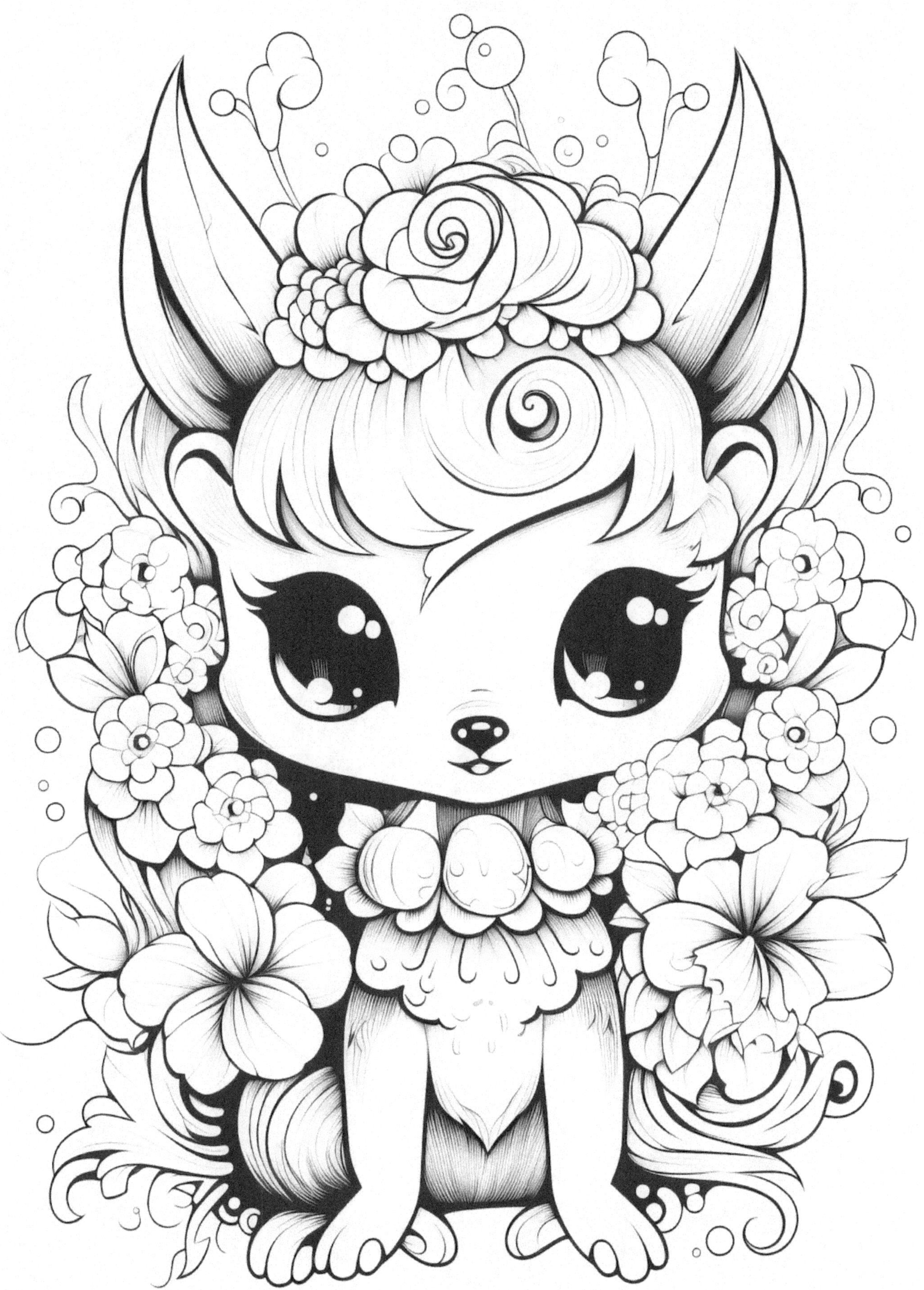

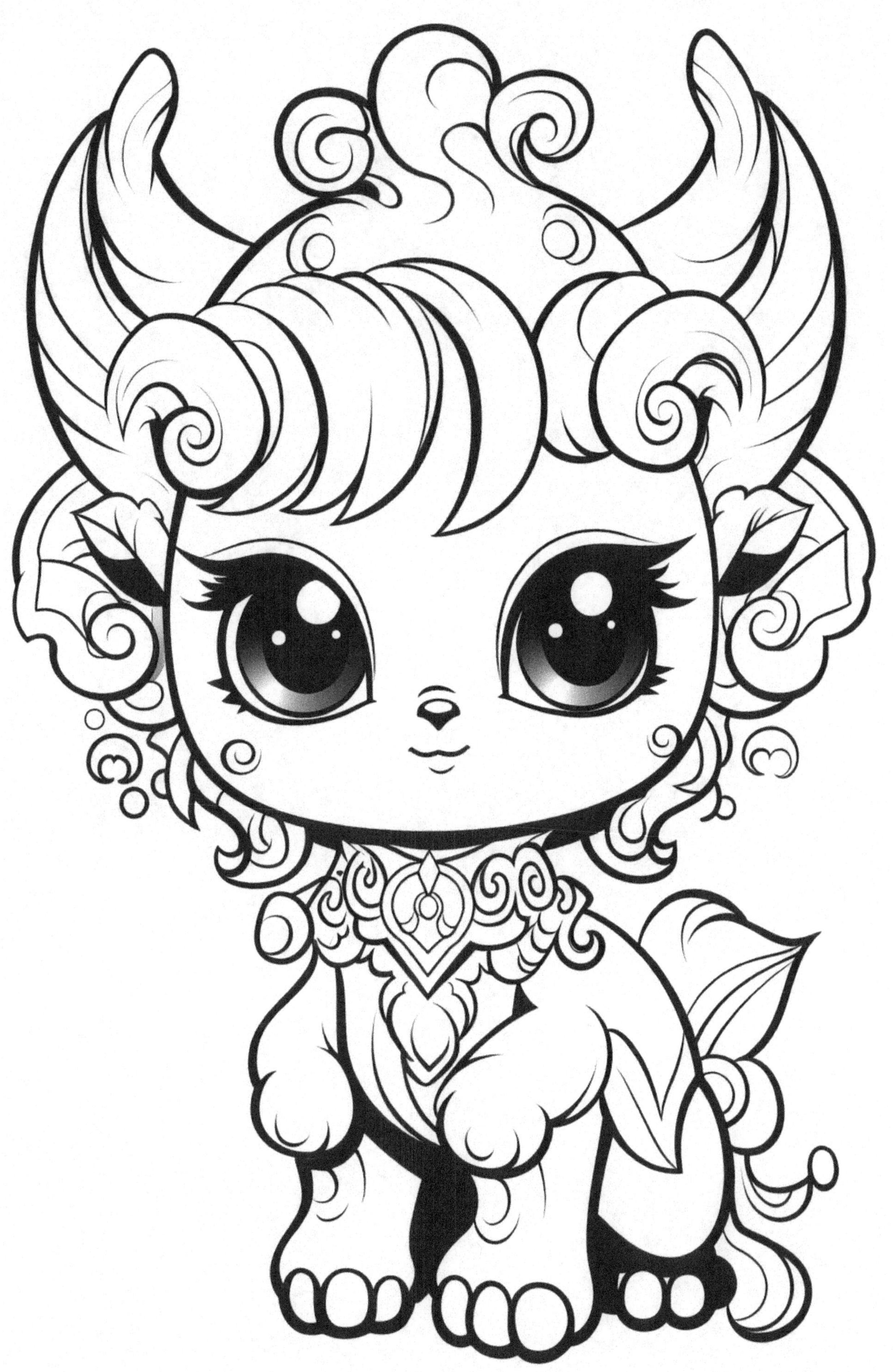

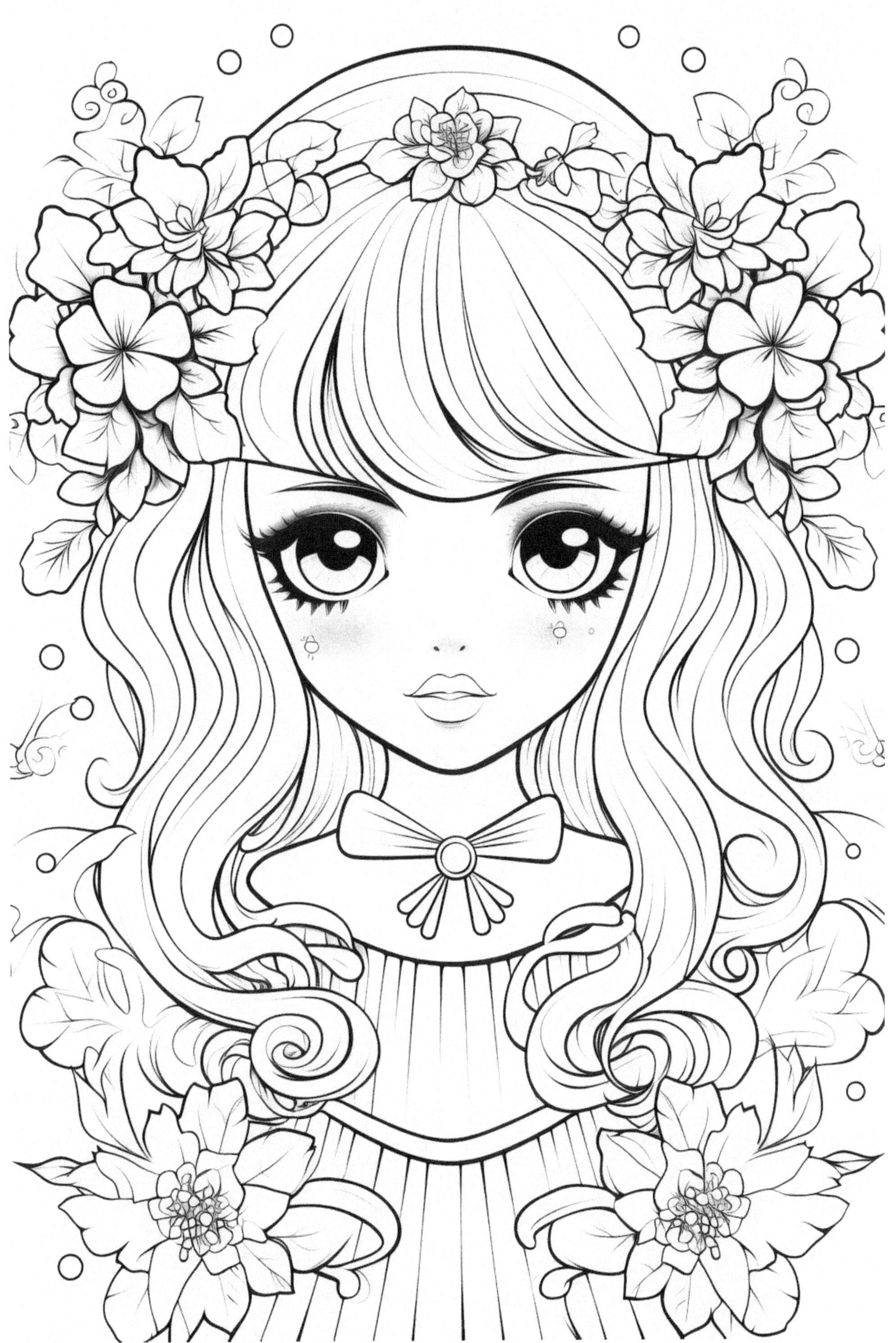

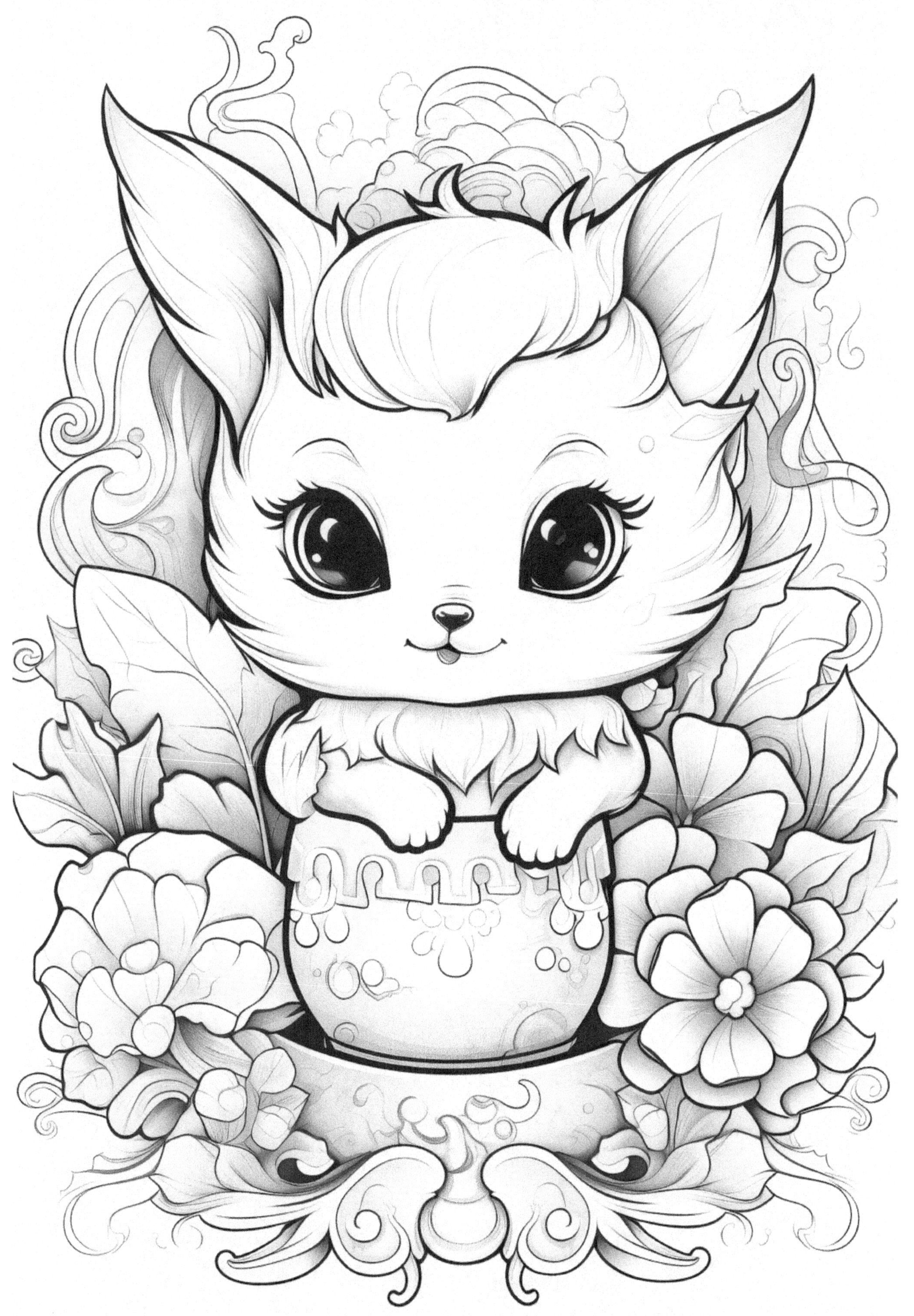

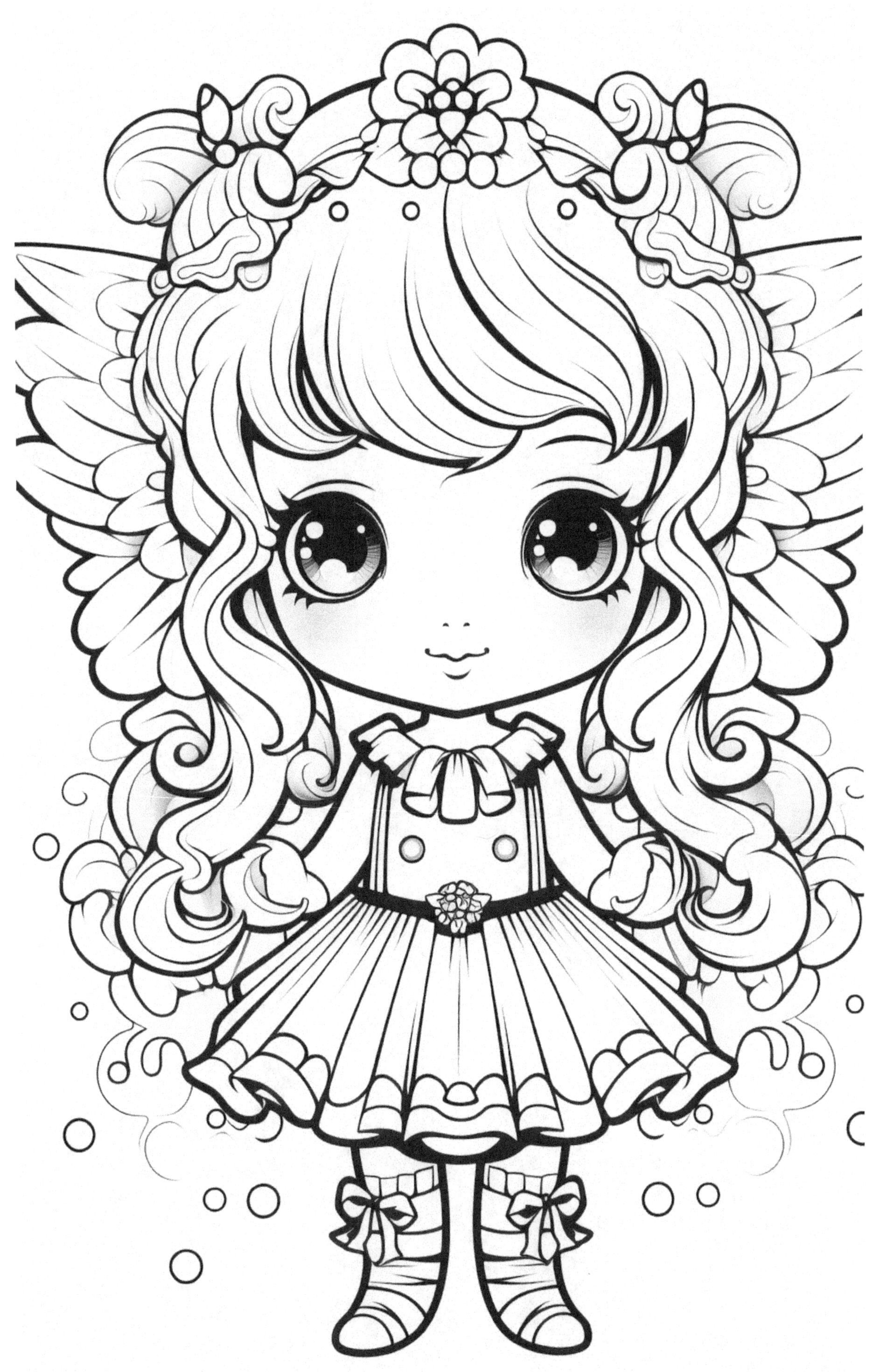

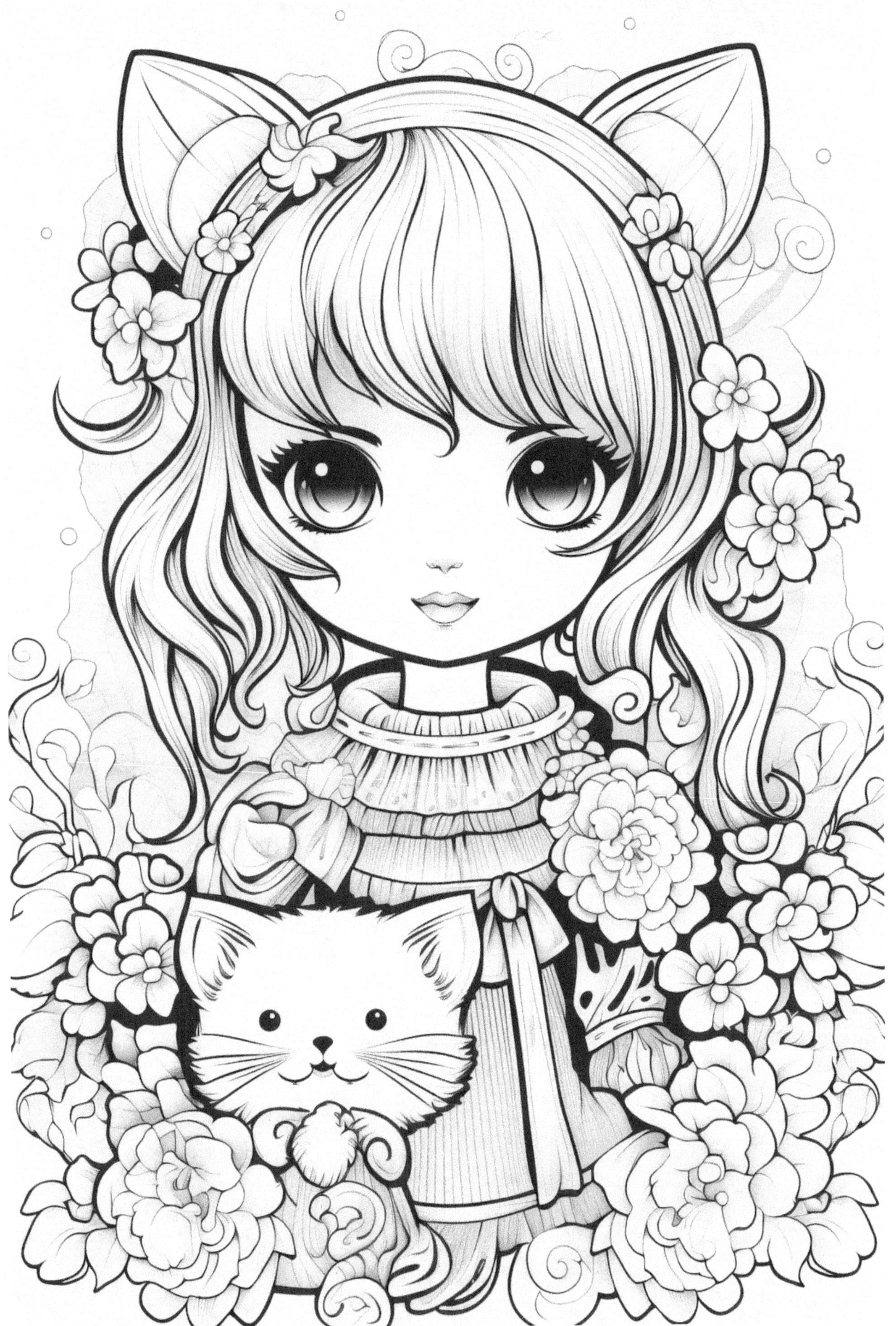

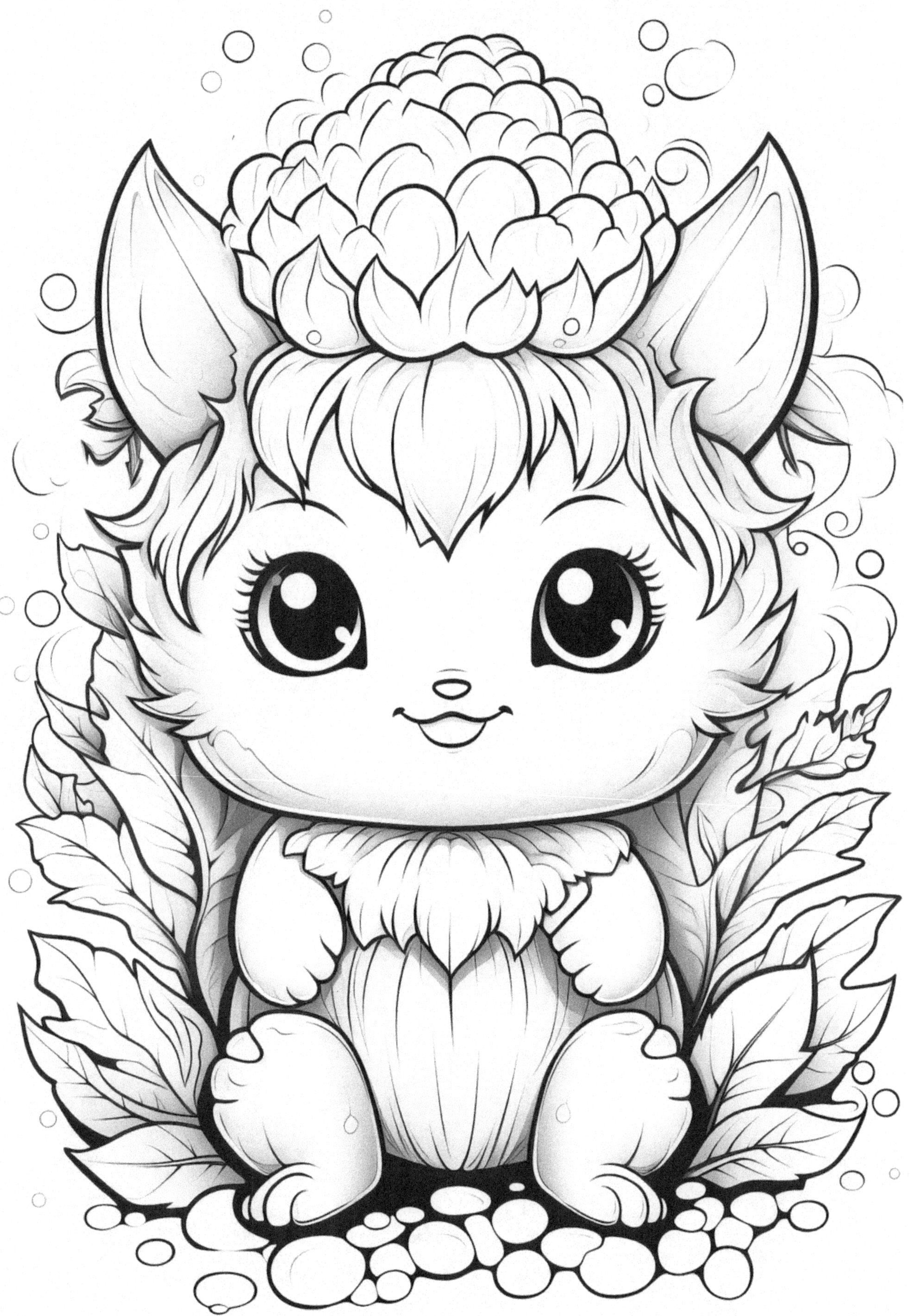

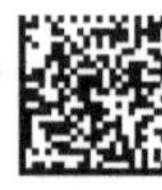